END BRITISH SUPPORT FOR ZIONISM
Isolate the Israeli state

▼ CONTENTS

a pamphlet by
FIGHT RACISM!
FIGHT IMPERIALISM!

An **FRFI** pamphlet

Published by Larkin Publications
BCM Box 5909, London, WC1N 3XX
©2024
www.frfi.org.uk

ISBN: 978-0-905400-33-4

Cover design: Séamus Ó Tuairisc
Design and typesetting: Joe Smith

INTRODUCTION
ISOLATE THE ZIONIST STATE

The Israeli military genocidal onslaught on the people of Palestine that has followed the 7 October action by the Palestinian resistance could have been predicted. It was the inevitable consequence of a brutal imperialist settlement imposed on the Palestinian people in 1948 by Britain in support of the newly-established Zionist state of Israel.

The Revolutionary Communist Group has long recognised that this essentially racist colonising strategy could never be accepted by the Palestinians. Despite repeated collusion and betrayal by their supposed representatives in the Palestinian Authority, Palestinian resistance has never stopped. Endlessly punished by enforced refugee status, the repeated imprisonment of nearly one fifth of the population, unceasing arbitrary murders, banishment, and the destruction of land, houses, water, communities and culture, resistance survives. At the same time the Zionist state, supported and financed by imperialism, has continued its territorial expansion based on a reactionary ideological mix of Biblical rights, theocratic law, and claims that it is 'the only democracy in the Middle East.'

With the creation of the Zionist state in 1948, the British established what the first British Governor of Jerusalem had called in 1917 'a little loyal Jewish Ulster', a launching pad for imperialist interests throughout the Middle East. Support for Israel is support for reaction. Not only is the Zionist state an apartheid state based on the overtly racist belief in the superiority of the Jewish people, but it also stands armed with the most modern weaponry, supports the most oppressive regimes, and has consistently stood against liberation struggles and movements for socialism.

The Palestinians, in contrast, have no army. Over the last 75 years, they have been in receipt of placatory donations from the EU and US to maintain a state of dependency. NGOs have built hospitals and schools while the United Nations has tried feebly to protect their few rights. In Britain, the Palestine Solidarity Campaign has been a fringe interest for members on the left of the Labour Party. The existence of the Zionist state as such has almost never been questioned.

The powerful Zionist lobby has always been watchful and active. At any point where criticism of Israel has reached a certain level it has launched a fierce double attack on its critics as both anti-Semitic and opposed to western imperialist interests. To silence critics and institutionalise protection of Zionism, the International Holocaust Remembrance Alliance published a definition of anti-Semitism in 2016, which deliberately conflates criticism of Israel with criticism of the Jewish people, that is, anti-Zionism with anti-Semitism. Under Jeremy Corbyn's leadership, the Labour Party accepted the definition. This surrender to Zionism, however, did not stem the torrent of spurious allegations that Corbyn had presided over a massive rise in anti-Semitism within the Labour Party. In the end, the Zionist campaign, relentlessly amplified by the mainstream media, was a major factor in sweeping him from the Labour leadership.

Working class people in Britain, many of Muslim background, have taken to the streets repeatedly in their hundreds of thousands calling for an end to the bombing of Gaza and demanding an end to the Zionist occupation of Palestinian land. They have condemned the stance of the Labour Party leadership in refusing to support a ceasefire, and Labour Party candidates will deservedly lose future elections because they allowed the ferocious bombing of homes, schools and hospitals in Gaza to continue unimpeded.

For the Revolutionary Communist Group, the immediate objectives of solidarity must be to oppose any imperialist plans for Palestine and to enforce the isolation of the Zionist state. We stand by the right of the Palestinian people to determine their own future. But while the Palestinian people directly confront the Zionist state, socialists and communists in Britain do not. Our principal enemy is the British imperialist state, and our task is to break its alliance with Zionism. That would be our most effective solidarity with the Palestinian people, and it must continue after any ceasefire.

Many of the articles in this pamphlet first appeared in *Fight Racism! Fight Imperialism!* They show the historical extent of our support for the Palestinian people: we have always seen the fight against Zionism as vital to building a socialist, anti-imperialist movement in this country. And our support is not just words: we organise marches, pickets, street events, public meetings, and we constantly expose the Labour Party because of its imperialist and Zionist character. Our paper stands for the defeat of British imperialism and for socialism. We urge you to join us.

chapter one

PALESTINE RESISTS

▼ by *Louis Brehony*
from *FRFI No.297*, December 2023/January 2024

The brutal siege and military invasion of al-Shifa hospital in Gaza city epitomised the Zionist assault on this most steadfast region of colonised Palestine, attempting to violently redress the humiliating defeat inflicted on Israeli military machinery on 7 October 2023. Backed to the hilt by ultra-rich imperialist states, and throwing every possible form of weaponry at a largely unarmed people, the occupation has sought to drown the Palestinian resistance in blood. But, while they have razed Gaza neighbourhoods, the four-day ceasefire scheduled for 24 November was a significant setback for the Zionist state and its imperialist supporters.

Israeli government ministers make no effort to hide their genocidal intentions. Avi Dichter declared on 11 November that 'we are now rolling out the Gaza Nakba', in reference to the 1948 ethnic cleansing which removed 750,000 Palestinians to make way for the Zionist state. Yet, the Zionists have failed to defeat the Palestinian resistance and those who fight alongside it, and have had to negotiate with them.

Resigning on 28 October, former New York UNHCR director Craig Mokhiber condemned US and European powers as 'wholly complicit in the horrific assault.' With 'genocide unfolding before our eyes,' the UN had once again proven incapable of standing on the side of justice. 1.2 million people had been displaced; more than half of all homes in Gaza had been destroyed by Zionist bombs; running water had been cut off by the occupation since 9 October and finding it had become 'like prospecting for gold,' according to *We Are Not Numbers*; besieged and bombed hospitals were running at 200% capacity; and the Palestinian population faced hourly massacres, with children killed in overwhelming numbers.

As we go to press, over 15,000 Palestinians have been killed in Zionist attacks, including 6,000 children. The true number is thousands more, with unknown numbers of bodies trapped under the rubble. Already, on 9 October, Jens Laerke, UN humanitarian affairs director had stated, 'If there is a hell on earth, it is the north of Gaza'. Vast swathes are now dust, bombed and bulldozed as Israeli troops film themselves desecrating schools and children's bedrooms. Having instructed the population of northern Gaza to 'evacuate' south, on 17 November the Zionists then bombed the southern Khan Younis refugee camp, the historic 'castle of revolution', warning hundreds of thousands more to leave. Many will remain.

In a deliberate and systematic campaign, the Israeli military is targeting all civilian infrastructure, from housing and bakeries, to water and energy. The most dire of this litany of crimes is the sledgehammer destruction of Gaza's already blockaded and starved healthcare system. 230 attacks on hospitals and healthcare centres had been documented by 11 November, with 704 healthcare workers and patients killed, and 71% of primary care centres put out of action, including 18 hospitals completely ceasing to operate.

Witnessing an intensified campaign from 9 November, Dar al-Shifa hospital faced a crippling and sustained attack at the hands of Zionist forces. Its cardiac ward was bombed and destroyed, fleeing healthcare workers shot and the hospital was subject to a constant siege. On 11 November three of 39 babies held in intensive care died immediately as they were taken out of incubators, inoperable due to the fuel blockade and ongoing attacks. Numbers of newborns requiring intensive care have risen sharply as a result of the Zionist bombing, including babies hit in the bombing, as well as those orphaned with the killing of entire families.

Mass graves were dug within the hospital grounds and over 170 buried. Preparing the invasion of al-Shifa, Israeli tanks were stationed at the hospital's gates while snipers and drones fired into the main compound. On 13 November, four patients and two nurses were killed by these snipers and the following night Israeli troops entered the compound. In language repeated by reactionaries internationally, from US president Biden to the British *Guardian* newspaper, the occupation claimed that underneath al-Shifa was a Hamas command centre, with tunnels and weapons caches on site.

Continuing a cowardly campaign of communications blackouts, the Zionists spent the next four days 'investigating' inside the hospital. 7,000 people – patients and healthcare workers – were trapped as the invaders turned al-Shifa into 'a detention camp, an interrogation centre, a military barracks and mass grave,' according to hospital spokesperson Ismail al-Thawabta. On 18 November, the invaders delivered orders to evacuate the hospital, sparking a panicked rush among severely injured and critically ill patients. Director General of Gaza hospitals Mohammed Zaqout confirmed that 'we were forced to leave at gunpoint'. Needless to say, the Zionists found nothing at al-Shifa. They nevertheless detained vulnerable patients at seven-hour checkpoints during their evacuation on 22 November, and seized al-Shifa director Muhamad Abu Salmiya, who had insisted on remaining with the injured. Reporting on 14 November, Human Rights Watch – itself no friend of the resistance – found 'no evidence' for Israeli claims that Hamas had been using hospitals in any way and called for the International Criminal Court to investigate Israel for war crimes.

Beyond the walls of al-Shifa, the Gaza Strip has burned under imperialist-sponsored Zionist massacres by fighter jets provided by US companies Lockheed Martin and Boeing. Britain contributes 15% of the components to US-supplied F-35 aircraft, used extensively over Gaza, and has exported £472m worth of arms to the Zionist state since 2015. On 31 October, these warplanes dropped two bombs weighing over 900kg at Jabaliya refugee camp. Over 200 were killed in two days of massacres, which destroyed residential buildings and the families inside. Jabaliya has remained a site of terror and resistance, with other massacres occurring on 22 October, and 13, 19 and 22 November. Among these terrorist attacks on 19 November, the Zionists bombed al-Fakhoura school, killing over 200, mostly displaced children and women. On 21 November, with the ceasefire all but agreed, the Zionists hammered Jabaliya again, simultaneously killing Palestinians in Rafah and Khan Younis. Such are the consequences of 'Israel's right to defend itself'.

War, resistance and unending imperialist-Zionist crisis

The Zionist onslaught has failed in its objectives, with no sign that Hamas or any other resistance faction has been seriously weakened by the war. Acts of resistance take place daily, with anti-tank missiles targeting military vehicles within the Gaza Strip and over its north and eastern 'borders.' Halting a wider ground invasion, fire fights take place in historic and newly established centres of struggle, in the camps, urban centres and rural zones. Despite well over a month of Zionist warfare, retaliatory rockets have continued to launch from Gaza.

There are also no signs that the Zionist brutality will succeed in quelling fierce resistance in Jenin, Nablus, Tulkarem and other areas of the occupied West Bank. Despite the puppet Palestinian Authority (PA) setting its forces on protesters – many of whom chant for 'the fall of the president', Mahmoud Abbas – mobilisations are gathering pace. These forces confront the Zionists' acceleration of land-grabs, as fascist ministers arm colonial settlers and stoke further violent colonisation. From 7 October to 22 November, at least 225 Palestinians were killed in the West Bank amidst a campaign of mass arrests, while Zionist planes flattened buildings in Jenin and Ramallah. What happens in Jenin, writes Ramallah-based journalist Fayha Shalash, 'resembles the aggression against Gaza, as well as the unsuccessful attempts to silence the resistance'.

The targets in Gaza are the Palestinian people as a whole, and whichever of their organisations stand on the side of the resistance, whether Hamas, Islamic Jihad, PFLP, DFLP or Fatah. They are joined by internationalist forces from Lebanon, Syria, Iraq and Yemen, multiplying the impossible

The Great Return March, April 2018, Gaza

mission waged by the Zionist state. Zionist embassies have been firebombed in Jordan and Bahrain but, during the 11-12 November Arab League summit, Saudi Arabia and Jordan led the vetoing of proposals to break ties with the Zionist state.

The US government has set no serious constraints on the Israeli state, its attack dog. Acknowledging on 15 November that Israeli methods are 'indiscriminate,' President Biden nevertheless virulently opposed UN ceasefire calls. An identical position is taken by Britain's Conservative government and Labour 'opposition'. Zionist military spokesperson Amir Avivi told BBC Newsnight on 13 October, Palestinians in Gaza 'need to move south, out to the Sinai peninsula.' This mass population transfer is seriously being considered by the Zionists, as shown in a 'concept paper' whose alternatives included rule by an Arab regime or a PA takeover of the Gaza Strip. Careful to balance their alliances with Egypt and other regional bourgeoisies, and fearful of much broader resistance, US imperialism and its allies have chosen the latter option. The desperation of this position is reflected in the fact that the hugely unpopular PA has proven incapable of governing even its Ramallah fiefdom.

Imperialist rivalries are bubbling beneath the surface, with cracks appearing in US-EU relations. The Belgian government has called for targeted sanctions against Israel while, on 10 November, France's President Macron said, uncharacteristically, there was 'no legitimacy' in the shelling of children and civilians. There is unease in European corridors of power, with 850 EU staff signing a letter criticising President Ursula von der Leyen's unconditional support for Israel. Imperialism is seething in economic and political contradictions.

The Zionist state itself faces a crisis on all levels. War cabinet minister Benny Gantz said on 8 November that, 'The war here is for our existence and for Zionism', with 'no limitations' on its duration. Though Netanyahu has pulled together a ragtag regime of hawks and open fascists, his rule and strategy are opposed by significant sections of Israeli society. Angry at corruption and a failure to release Israeli captives, a group of families organised a march on the home of Netanyahu on 14 November, as many others called for negotiations. Hamas' repeated offers of the release of Zionist hostages in exchange for a limited ceasefire were ignored by the occupation. This eventually changed with a Qatar-brokered deal which would see a four-day humanitarian truce from 24 November, whereby around 150 Palestinian prisoners would be released in exchange for 50 of those captured in Israel, and 200 aid trucks allowed into Gaza, along with four daily trucks of fuel and cooking gas. The Zionist state and its imperialist backers have been forced to accept this ceasefire by the campaign of Palestinian armed struggle.

Tactical ceasefire calls on the part of the Palestinian resistance are substantially different to the liberal demands of Western campaigners. As put by Khaled Barakat of Samidoun, with 'people being subjugated to ethnic cleansing and genocide, if you ask them to stop their fire, it's just misleading.' The stated aim of this Zionist war is the total liquidation of the Palestinian forces of resistance. This goal has been at the heart of imperialist interventions in Palestine since Britain sent troops to Jerusalem in 1917, and applied the most brutal of its colonial counterinsurgency tactics to crush the Palestinian revolution of 1936-39.

Speaking on 15 October, PFLP central committee member Leila Khaled exposed the empty language of international law and Security Council resolutions. The UN, she said, is 'the power of the oppressors, the capitalists, the imperialists and the Zionists.' Calling for Palestinian armed resistance to be the basis of a global movement, she pointed to the crisis at the heart of the imperialist camp: 'They fear us and this is important, to change the balance of forces. Let them fear [us] everywhere.'

chapter two

LABOUR DEFENDS GENOCIDE

▼ by *Robert Clough*
from *FRFI No.297*, December 2023/January 2024

The outrage that followed the refusal of the Labour Party leadership to back the call for a ceasefire in the parliamentary vote on 15 November 2023 was inevitable: it was the final straw for hundreds of thousands of people who had been demonstrating against the blitzkrieg on Palestine. Throughout the war, the Labour Party has sided with the Zionist state and deliberately ignored all the prima face evidence of Zionist war crimes and of its genocidal intent. Instead, leader Sir Keir Starmer gave a green light to collective punishment of the people of Gaza, blaming the suffering of the Palestinian people on the 7 October 2023 military action of the resistance forces. It shows once again that the Labour Party is first and foremost an imperialist party. It has to defend the interests of British imperialism and that means it will never abandon its Zionist ally, the guarantor of Britain's interests in the Middle East.

The 15 November vote was preceded by a huge demonstration numbering over half a million which took place on Armistice Day, 11 November, despite the outrage of the Tory government and the racist tabloids. The Metropolitan Police rejected calls to ban the march, fully aware that they would face open defiance from tens of thousands of people; the Labour leadership evaded taking sides by saying it was an operational question for the Met. Following the ceasefire debacle, anger reached a new pitch, and demonstrations took place outside several

Labour Party offices in the constituencies of MPs who had refused to back the amendment. Hundreds had already protested against the arch-Zionist Shadow Health Secretary Wes Streeting, besieging the Labour Party offices in his Ilford North constituency on 6 November. The following day, Year 13 pupils walked out of assembly at the local Beal High School because Streeting was due to attend it; at the same time, primary and secondary school students walked out in Bristol.

'Labour Party - shame on you'

The day after the House of Commons vote, crowds led by school students demonstrated outside the office of Bethnal Green and Bow MP Rushanara Ali, chanting 'vote her out' and 'Labour Party shame on you' because she would not support the ceasefire vote. Over the next few days there were protests in further Labour-held constituencies including a demonstration outside Starmer's offices. Other protests have taken place outside a surgery held by Steve McCabe, the Labour MP for Birmingham Selly Oak, with crowds chanting 'Steve McCabe, you can't hide, you're supporting genocide.' It was reported that he tried to escape in his Porsche SUV. Shabana Mahmodd from nearby Birmingham Ladywood was also targeted, as was Shadow Attorney General Emily Thornberry.

These demonstrations have brought predictable outrage from Labour leaders: Harriet Harman condemned the spraying of slogans on Shadow Welsh Secretary Jo Stevens' office as 'an attack on democracy'; Shadow Chancellor Rachel Reeves declared 'I believe in the right to protest, I don't believe in the right to intimidate. Some of those protests, I believe, over the last few days have crossed the line from protest to intimidation. Protesting outside people's homes, putting pressure on them in that way, I think it's totally unacceptable.' There is no evidence that any protest has taken place outside an MP's home.

Labour defends war crimes

The protesters' anger is fully justified. Day after day, week after week following the 7 October action by the Palestinian resistance, TV screens showed the Zionist war machine commit war crime after war crime: the use of phosphorus bombs, the forced expulsion of one million Palestinians from their homes in the north of Gaza, the bombing of schools and hospitals, the attacks on UN premises, the invasions of hospitals and seizure of male patients. Yet Starmer's response was to insist that 'It's unwise for politicians to stand on stages like this or to sit in television studios and pronounce day by day which acts may or may not be lawful under international law.' He also said a ceasefire would 'freeze the conflict', allowing Hamas to launch attacks against Israel again in the future. 'Hamas would be emboldened and start preparing for future violence immediately.'

Starmer's determination to stand in unconditional defence of the Zionist terror campaign was evident from its outset. He condemned the 7 October resistance action immediately as a 'massacre' undertaken by 'terrorists' against which the Zionist state had every right to retaliate under the claim to 'self-defence'. Asked whether the Zionist state had the right to cut off food and water supplies as it was threatening to do, he replied in an interview on 11 October 'I think that Israel does have that right, it is an ongoing situation, obviously everything should be done within international law but I don't want to step away from the core principles that Israel has the right to defend herself.'

Suggesting that such collective punishment, a war crime, could be within international law required a logic known only to himself. It took three weeks for him to attempt to row back from these comments, by which time it was too late for anyone to believe that he was not giving a green light to genocide. Not once has he suggested that the Palestinian people have the right to defend themselves. By that time, Labour had suspended MP Andy McDonald for 'deeply offensive' comments at a pro-Palestine rally on 28 October; his offence was a completely anodyne declaration that 'We will not rest until we have justice. Until all people, Israelis and Palestinians, between the river and the sea, can live in peaceful liberty.'

Nandy: Israel first

Starmer was not alone among senior Labour politicians in standing four-square with the Zionist terror. The day after the ceasefire vote, the Shadow International Development Secretary Lisa Nandy reiterated where Labour Party priorities lay, saying that 'To many people in Israel, including the Israeli government, when they hear the term ceasefire it is simply an instruction that they should lay down their arms and just allow that situation to continue. I don't see how that's a correct position to hold.' Such a declaration, made at the same time as Zionist forces were scouring Al Shifa hospital for alleged Hamas tunnels, and while patients were dying in the intensive care unit, shows the barbaric character of the Labour leadership. Its prime concern throughout has been to protect the interests of its Zionist attack dog.

While the protests outside Labour Party offices have focused on those who failed to support the ceasefire vote, those who voted in favour cannot be seen as less reactionary. The amendment to the King's Speech that they supported included the statement that they 'unequivocally condemn the horrific killings by Hamas and the taking of hostages' but pointedly did not equally 'unequivocally condemn' any actions which were part of the Zionist blitzkrieg. Not a single Labour MP has expressed any support for Palestinian resistance; an Early Day Motion organised by left Labour MPs in the Socialist Campaign Group on 17 October 'utterly condemns the massacre of Israeli civilians and taking of hostages by Hamas'. There was no equivalent condemnation of the numerous war crimes that the Zionist state had already committed. John McDonnell damned the 7 October operation as 'the killing of the innocents by Hamas', despite evidence that the cause of many deaths was indiscriminate fire from Israeli attack helicopters. Support for a ceasefire is to be the limit of any 'revolt' against the Starmer leadership; questioning the legitimacy of the Zionist state, let alone its relationship with the British imperialist state, is complete anathema.

Corbyn condemns Palestinian resistance

The behaviour of Jeremy Corbyn throughout these weeks has been abject. Despite knowing that he will not be allowed to stand as a Labour MP at the next election, he has refused to criticise the stance of the Labour leadership or directly challenge Starmer for his endorsement of the Zionist military onslaught. At the first national Palestine Solidarity Campaign (PSC) demonstration on 14 October he told the crowd that the solution to the crisis was to uphold international law, that 'the horrific attacks on civilians in Israel were deplorable', and that 'none of us are here to condone killing.' But not a word of criticism of Starmer passed his lips.

Later, on Piers Morgan's TalkTV show, he came across as weak and evasive as he was repeatedly challenged over his attitude to Hamas. But in The Tribune a few days later he would write that 'if we understand terrorism to describe the indiscriminate killing of civilians, in breach of international law, then Hamas is a terrorist group' and that he had 'repeatedly condemned' the Hamas attack 'in Parliament, in print and at every demonstration I have attended'. Yet still he refused to condemn Starmer, despite the latter saying that Corbyn's days as a Labour MP are over. Once again, as he has done so often in the past, Corbyn has placed his loyalty to the Labour Party before political principle.

The political impotence of the left of the Labour Party has rarely been more evident than at the present. It is terrified of attacking Starmer – he has isolated it as a credible force within the party. Either they knuckle under, or they have to go, and for left MPs that is a decision about their £86,000 a year jobs. Their hope is to salvage some electoral credibility with their stance over the ceasefire, and the PSC leadership is helping them out by giving them platforms on their demonstrations. Yet on the critical issue, the Labour left and the leadership are as one: there can be no rupture in the alliance between British imperialism and the Zionist state. That is why the protests outside Labour Party offices are so significant: for the first time in decades, a section of the working class is starting to oppose Labour. It is a move that socialists and communists must foster by attacking the legitimacy of the Zionist state and demanding its total isolation through the imposition of economic, political, diplomatic and cultural sanctions. With the legion of war crimes committed by the Zionist state over the past few weeks, its plans to complete the genocide of the Palestinian people, it is the minimum stand we can take to support the right of the Palestinian people to self-determination.

18 November 2023, protest outside HSBC Oxford Street, London

Trade unions – toeing the Zionist line

While trade union leaders are obligatory speakers on both national and local demonstration platforms, not a single union has made a progressive statement on the war. Unite speaks of 'crimes committed by Hamas'; Unison of 'a brutal and heinous attack that has claimed the lives of many hundreds of innocent civilians' that has 'devastated' Israel; Universities and Colleges Union condemned 'in the strongest possible terms the targeting of civilian life by both Israeli military and Hamas.' The TUC said 'We unequivocally condemn the attacks by Hamas and their targeting of civilians in this recent escalation of violence. Nothing can justify such an attack.' For them, the right of the Palestinian people to resist does not exist.

chapter three

GAZA RESISTS ISRAELI OCCUPATION

by *Bob Shepherd*
from *FRFI No.297*, December 2023/January 2024

The death and destruction that Israel has rained down on Gaza since 7 October, the deliberate targeting of residential areas, of hospitals, mosques and schools, is the latest and most brutal attempt at the destruction and ethnic cleansing of Gaza. Since the 2006 election victory of Hamas, the Israeli state, supported by the US, Britain and the EU, has been determined to make the Palestinian people pay for their continued resistance to the Zionist state.

Gaza is a strip of land approximately 25 miles long and five miles wide. Before the latest barbaric onslaught it had a population of around 2.3 million, the vast majority of whom are descendants of refugees forced from their homes in 1948 by the Zionist terror squads. More than half of the population are under 18 years old.

In his book *Gaza: An inquest into its martyrdom,* Norman Finkelstein documented the history of Zionist terrorism in Gaza from 1948 up to and including the so-called Operation Protective Edge in 2014 (see our review on www.frfi.org.uk). The book details the death and destruction meted out by Israel in both the 2008/09 Operation Cast Lead and the 2014 Operation Protective Edge, exposing the hypocrisy of the UN, Amnesty International and Human Rights Watch in covering up for Israel's war crimes.

After the 1967 war Israel occupied Gaza, built a number of colonial settlements and kept it under tight military control until 2005 when it pulled out its settlers and troops, beginning the economic blockade, continuously tightened ever since. In 2006, in a rejection of the rampant corruption of the Palestinian Authority (PA) Hamas won a majority in the Palestinian elections that were described by former US President Jimmy Carter as 'completely honest and fair'. The response of Israel, supported by the US, Britain and the EU was to impose even tougher economic sanctions on Gaza.

In 2007, Hamas defeated a coup attempt by elements of Fatah in Gaza which had been instigated by the PA in alliance with the Zionist state, Britain and the US. The Zionists tightened the screw even further. According to a United Nations study, by January 2008 electricity was being provided for less than eight hours a day, water supplies connected only once a week with 80% unfit for human consumption, food security and medical supplies were at an all-time low.

At least 158 non-combatants had already been killed in Israeli military strikes during 2008 by the time Operation Cast Lead was launched on 27 December. The Zionist onslaught killed over 1,400 Palestinians, 80% of whom were civilians, including 350 children. Almost half of Gaza's 122 health facilities, including 15 hospitals, were damaged or demolished, and 16 medical personnel were killed. The two top floors of Al Quds Hospital were destroyed, Al Wafa and the European Hospitals in Khan Younis were hit by tank shells, missiles and thousands of bullets. Zionist forces razed or damaged 58,000 homes, 280 schools and six university buildings. Factories, agricultural centres, electrical, water and sewage facilities were also targeted. Tsipi Livni, then Israeli Foreign Minister, later declared that Cast Lead had 'restored Israel's deterrence... Hamas now understands that when you fire on Israel's citizens it responds by going wild – and this is a good thing... Israel demonstrated real hooliganism'.

In 2009, the Goldstone Report was published as the culmination of a UN Human Rights Council 'fact finding mission' to investigate violations of human rights during Cast Lead. Goldstone was a former judge of the Constitutional Court of South Africa and a Zionist, but his report, Finkelstein writes, was 'a searing indictment not just of Cast Lead but also of the ongoing Israeli occupation'. The report found that much of the destruction carried out by Israel had been premeditated, and concluded that the Israeli assault constituted 'a deliberately disproportionate attack designed to punish, humiliate and terrorise a civilian population, radically diminish its local economic capacity both to work and to provide for itself, and to force upon it an ever increasing sense of dependency and vulnerability'. These were war crimes.h

As expected, the report prompted a torrent of abuse across the Zionist political spectrum as well as defenders of the Zionist state internationally. The US under President Obama led the attack, while the PA refused to push the issue within UN bodies. Then on 1 April 2011, Goldstone distanced himself from the report he had written. The consequence of his action became evident in 2014 when no major human rights organisation was prepared to point the finger at Israel for the crimes that it committed under Operation Protective Edge.

Protective Edge was launched by Israel on 8 July 2014 and lasted 51 days, leaving more than 1,500 civilians dead, including 550 children. Israel fired 20,000 high explosive artillery shells, 14,500 tank shells, 6,000 missiles and 3,500 naval shells into Gaza during this period, destroying 18,000 homes. The President of the International Committee of the Red Cross is quoted after touring Gaza: 'I've never seen such massive destruction before.'

Since 2014 the Zionist state has launched other military operations in Gaza, most notably in May 2021 when over 250 Palestinians were killed after the resistance in Gaza responded to Zionist attacks on worshippers at the Al Aqsa Mosque in Jerusalem. Three years beforehand, activists organised the peaceful Great March of Return where thousands of people marched every Friday near to the Gazan border fences demanding the right for refugees to return to Palestine. 30,000 people supported the first demonstration on 30 March 2018; Israeli border guards used live ammunition and killed 15 demonstrators. By the end of 2018 at least 183 demonstrators had been shot and killed and over 9,000 injured.

The Palestinian people of Gaza have a long history of resistance to the Zionist occupation; this latest barbaric onslaught indicates Zionist intentions to ethnically cleanse Gaza of its Palestinian population.

Photo credit: @photographeroffortune

chapter four

BRITISH MEDIA SUPPORTS ZIONIST GENOCIDE

by *Ria Aibhilin*
from *FRFI No.297*, December 2023/January 2024

The Zionist onslaught on Gaza has been unequivocally backed by the British media establishment. Despite their best efforts, the British media, from the tabloids to the supposedly liberal *Guardian* and *Independent* and the 'impartial' BBC, have utterly failed to manufacture public consent for Israel's genocidal war against the Palestinian people, with their blatant lies exposed by the daily evidence of the Zionist state's war crimes.

Every major newspaper in Britain covered the events of 7 October as front page news. For weeks we were told 1,400 Israelis had been killed that day. Within 24 hours Zionist forces had murdered almost 250 Palestinians in indiscriminate attacks. 'Israel says "hundreds of terrorists dead"' *The Guardian* online headline told us (8 October). For the British media, Israelis are victims with names and stories, worthy of our attention and sympathy; Palestinians are just terrorists used to dying. Shameless racism is employed to dehumanise the Palestinian people.

The Guardian, with its historically 'left' readership, has played a particular role: 'propaganda is most effective when our consent is engineered by those with a fine education – Oxford, Cambridge, Harvard, Columbia – and with careers on the BBC, *The Guardian*, the *New York Times*, the Washington Post' (John Pilger, cited in *Propaganda Blitz*, p159). *The Guardian* has lined up the usual suspects to try to justify Israel's massacre of the Palestinian people in Gaza:

- As Zionist forces bombed the entrapped population in Gaza and starved its two million inhabitants of fuel, food and water, columnist George Monboit tried to kid us that this is an 'Israel-Hamas conflict' (18 October). Israeli ministers have openly declared it is 'rolling out the Gaza Nakba' and boasted 'Gaza Nakba 2023. That's how it'll end'.

- For Owen Jones, Israel's military onslaught was 'the aftermath of Hamas' unjustifiable atrocity' (24 October). From his acceptance of the Zionist framing, you would believe history began on 7 October. There is no mention of the illegal land, sea and air blockade imposed on Gaza since 2006, or of the mass expulsion of Palestinians from their homes and lands, the ongoing occupation of Palestine by the settler-colonial state of Israel or of the years of unending terror and violence inflicted on Palestinian people at the hands of Israeli forces. There is no mention of the 2,070 Palestinians, many of them children, held in administrative detention in the Israeli state before a single Israeli prisoner was taken on 7 October.

- When the story that Palestinian militants were beheading Israeli babies was revealed to be a lie, with even the IDF admitting it could not corroborate the claim made up on air by Nicole Zedeck of the i24News private Israeli channel, *The Guardian* did not want you to lose sympathy for the Zionist murder squads. Its Rory Carroll has often laid the groundwork for public support for foreign intervention in Latin America through spreading misinformation and lies. This time he spared his attention for an article detailing 'killings and mutilations during Hamas's rampage in southern Israel'. Only if you make it right to the very end of the article do you learn that in Israel's 'retaliatory bombing[s]' over 2,000 Palestinian children had been murdered before the publication of the article on 23 October, 'according to the Hamas-run health ministry'. Though figures provided by the Israeli state are quoted without qualification, suspicion and doubt is cast on the Hamas figures of Palestinian deaths.

As well as these *The Guardian* has:

• Erased the existence of Palestinians in the occupied 48 by racistly referring to them as 'Arabs in Israel' (20 October);

• Weaponised anti-Semitism by firing its cartoonist of 40 years, Steve Bell (Bell's sacking offence was a cartoon of Israeli Prime Minister Benjamin Netanyahu inspired by an old cartoon of former US President Lyndon Johnson); promoting the IHRA definition of anti-Semitism; running articles about pro-Palestine marches not being a 'comfortable environment for Jews' (18 November).

16 September 2023, Palestine Resists protest, BBC, London

Similarly, the BBC was forced to retract its misleading comments that marches in solidarity with Palestine are characterised by 'people voic[ing] their backing for Hamas'. The BBC and *The Guardian* quote statistics from the Zionist state without qualification. It doesn't matter to them that the figure of 1,400 Israeli deaths branded across every major news source was later announced by the IDF to be a lie. It doesn't matter that of the revised-down figure of 1,200 deaths over 350 of them were military personnel. It doesn't matter that an Israeli police investigation later found that some of the Israeli civilian casualties at the Supernova festival on 7 October were killed by the IDF attack helicopters.

On 16 November the BBC revealed the depths to which it is willing to go to defend the genocidal acts carried out by the Israeli state. While the Israeli state forces attacked the Al-Shifa hospital with bombs and snipers, imposed a siege on the hospital and cut it off from fuel, food, water and medical equipment; while Palestinians were being forced to have amputations and women to have C-sections without anaesthesia; while the life support machines keeping newborn babies alive were cut off and the Zionist forces targeted medical professionals and opened fire on patients, the BBC Question Time panel took the question: 'Is the Israeli targeting of a hospital justified?' The panellists overwhelmingly agreed it was. The targeting of hospitals is an international war crime. The BBC aired this unashamed promotion of mass slaughter to a portion of its eight million regular viewers.

Mainstream British media – the tabloids, *The Guardian*, the BBC – are the unofficial spokespersons of various sections of the British ruling class. They are united in defending its imperialist interests. From Ireland to Iraq, they have brazenly laid the groundwork for and justified the brutal consequences of the needs of British imperialism. We must not be fooled as they do so today to protect British foreign interests in the Middle East and around the globe.

13 January 2024, Global Day of Action for Gaza, Central London.

chapter five

20 YEARS OF INTIFADA

▼ by *Wesam Khaled*
from *FRFI No.278*, October/November 2020

28 September 2020 marked the 20th anniversary of the outbreak of the Al Aqsa Intifada, or Second Intifada, in September 2000. The Intifada saw millions of Palestinians fill the streets in a programme of mass demonstrations and civil disobedience to oppose Israel's occupation and programme of ethnic cleansing. Rejecting years of a one-sided 'peace process', the Palestinian people shook the Israeli state and shone a spotlight on the realities of the Israeli occupation. Israel's response to the uprisings was brutal and bloody, and was backed to the hilt by western imperialist powers including Britain's then-Labour government led by Tony Blair. Solidarity activists around the world supported the Palestinians in their struggle, including FRFI which organised constant events across Britain; but, then as now, those actions faced vilification and harassment not only from Zionists but from false friends of Palestine on the British left.

Origins of an uprising

The Intifada emerged out of the failure of the Oslo 'Peace Process' which started in 1993. The dynamism and resistance of the First Intifada (1987-1993) had forced Israel into negotiations with the Palestinian exiled leadership with the supposed aim of peace (see FRFI 266: Oslo's legacy – a disaster for the Palestinians). The agreement in Oslo between Israel and the Palestinian Liberation Organisation (PLO), led by Yasser Arafat, marked the beginning of this process. Palestinians were led up the garden path of negotiations with their oppressor-occupier, putting an end to the Intifada. But this peace process was predicated on the unilateral recognition of Israel's right to exist and a PLO commitment to non-violence, while the issues of Palestinian self-determination and Israeli violence went unaddressed. Arafat's desperation to secure a deal, however miserable, was key: his negotiations took place behind the backs of the internal leadership of the Intifada, which was appalled at the consequent betrayal.

By 2000 the consequences were clear. The negotiations had moved no closer to resolving the key issues for the Palestinian people, such as the right of return of Palestinian refugees or the illegal Israeli settlements in Palestinian territory. Quite the opposite: Israel's settlement expansion tripled during the post-Oslo years, and there was no change in the oppressive conditions of the Israeli occupation. This failed process culminated in the Camp David Summit in July 2000, where Arafat had to reject an Israeli proposal that would have confined Palestinians to a sham 'state' criss-crossed with Israeli-only roads and without any control over its borders. For Palestinians, such a pitiful outcome of years of negotiations proved the impossibility of reaching a settlement with the occupying power. With the 'peace process' in tatters, and Palestinian frustration at their oppressors' intransigence reaching a boiling point, Palestine was on the brink of a second uprising.

The Al Aqsa Intifada

The catalyst came on 28 September 2000 when Ariel Sharon, leader of Israel's right-wing Likud Party, took a contingent of 1,000 Israeli police to the Al Aqsa Mosque in Jerusalem. After the injustices and frustrations of the Oslo years, the Palestinian response to this provocation was swift and fierce: the following day, Palestinians gathered for a mass demonstration at the mosque. Israeli forces retaliated with lethal force, killing seven Palestinians and injuring over 200 more.

The revolt quickly spread throughout historic Palestine as people took to the streets en masse in a wave of protests and civil disobedience unseen since the First Intifada. The uprising became front-page news across the world as Palestinians forced their demands for freedom, justice and self-determination into the spotlight. Iconic images of Palestinian children throwing stones at Israeli tanks illustrated the character of the uprising as one of a largely defenceless and unarmed population courageously confronting one of the strongest military forces in the world.

Sharon's onslaught

The Israeli state responded with utter brutality. Within six months of the outbreak of the Intifada, Sharon was elected Prime Minister of Israel, signalling the atrocities that were to come. Sharon had been a general in the Israeli army, and had overseen the massacre of thousands of Palestinian refugees in the Sabra and Shatilah refugee camps in Lebanon in 1982. When he came to power, he promised to crush the Palestinian uprising within 100 days. In this he failed, but not for lack of trying. One of his earliest acts was to unleash a bloody assault on the Khan Yunis refugee camp in the Gaza Strip, then home to 60,000 refugees who lived in squalid conditions. This was followed the next year by the launch of Operation Defensive Shield, a large scale military operation which saw roughly 20,000 Israeli troops invade and occupy cities across the West Bank. The most notorious of these was the attack on Jenin, a refugee camp-cum-city, home to 13,000 displaced Palestinians, in April 2002. The Israeli army besieged the city, preventing anyone from leaving or entering, cut off water, electricity, food and medical supplies, and destroyed hundreds of buildings, often with people inside who were buried in the rubble: dozens of Palestinian men, women and children were killed.

The Palestinian people did not take these assaults lying down. Alongside non-violent forms of resistance the Palestinian people resumed violent forms of struggle that had been largely abandoned during the Oslo years. Palestinian fighters held their own in pitched street battles against well-armed Israeli soldiers. Inevitably, Palestinian casualties far outnumbered those on the Israeli side.

Imperialist support for the Zionists

Yet throughout the Intifada, western imperialist states and the international media framed Israel as the victim and Palestinians as the aggressor in these battles. Israeli casualties were highlighted while Palestinian casualties minimised, if mentioned at all. The nature of the Intifada itself – at its core an uprising of an unarmed and oppressed population against a heavily armed occupier – was obfuscated. In its place, Israel's assault on Palestinians was cast as a continuation of the post-9/11 'War on Terror'; Zionists made use of the rampant Islamophobic propaganda employed to justify imperialist interventions in Afghanistan and Iraq, and framed the Palestinian struggle as just another example of the 'uncivilised' Muslim world.

This included the then-Labour government of Tony Blair, which was shameless in its support for the Zionist state during the Intifada. Two days before the assault on Jenin, British Foreign Secretary Jack Straw defended Israel in an article in *The Guardian*, condemning Palestinian violence while glossing over the continued occupation and denial of Palestinian rights that gave rise to that violence in the first place. In 2004, the British government opposed the decision of the International Court of Justice to examine the legality of the apartheid wall Israel was building in the West Bank. The Labour government also took every step possible to cover up the murder of three British solidarity activists by Israeli soldiers and to prevent any justice being served for their deaths. In the words of the father of Tom Hurndall, one of the victims who had been shot by a sniper, 'at one point [the British government] were as obstructive as the Israelis'.

By the end of the uprisings in 2005, Israel had killed 4,166 Palestinians, including 886 children; disabled or maimed a further 3,530 Palestinians; imprisoned 8,600 Palestinians, including 288 children; demolished 7,761 homes and damaged another 93,842; confiscated 2.3 million dunums of Palestinian land; and uprooted over 1.3 million trees in Palestinian land. 1,100 Israelis were killed. Arafat died in 2004 after being besieged by Israeli forces at his compound in Ramallah. He was replaced by Mahmoud Abbas, an even more willing collaborator with Israel who remains in power today.

The British left: solidarity and selling out

In Britain, the Intifada was supported by a swell of grassroots actions opposing Israel's atrocities and the support it received from the Labour government. FRFI was no exception; through the campaign Victory to the Intifada (VTI), it helped organise a longstanding series of demonstrations against Marks and Spencer (M&S). Founded by Greenribbon, an independent group led by young Muslim women, the campaign against M&S targeted the company for its role in openly supporting the Zionist state.

29 May 2021, protest at Marks & Spencer's flagship store, Marble Arch, London.

The ties between M&S and Israel ran deep. In 1990, Lord Marcus Sieff, M&S's long-time chair, wrote that one of the company's long-term objectives was to aid Israel's economic development. In 1998, Israel's then-Prime Minister Benjamin Netanyahu granted M&S the Jubilee Award for individuals and organisations that have done the most to strengthen the Israeli economy. After the outbreak of the Intifada, an M&S spokesperson said 'we are as close to Israel as we have ever been', and the company was conducting £250m worth of trade with Israel annually. VTI joined forces with Greenribbon under the banner of the Boycott M&S campaign, forming a regular presence in front of M&S stores in cities across Britain from the start of the Second Intifada and lasting for over 10 years. Demonstrations were regularly targeted by an assortment of British and Zionist fascist organisations which attempted to intimidate or drown out the protesters. They also faced a barrage of attempts by police and local authorities to shut them down using public order laws.

The campaign also had to contend with the open opposition of the opportunists of the British left, including the Palestine Solidarity Campaign (PSC) and the Socialist Workers Party (SWP). Attempts to set up a regular M&S picket in Liverpool were attacked by the local SWP organiser for supposedly failing to seek the permission of the Liverpool left (meaning the SWP) to do so. PSC members and leaders went even further; one PSC member in Edinburgh hurled abuse at activists on an M&S demonstration and pulled petition boards out of the hands of members of the public, telling them not to sign them. PSC leaders openly discouraged people from supporting the campaign, committed as they were to the two-state solution supported by both the PLO and all wings of the Labour Party. At a meeting in 2006 the PSC National Secretary called the M&S events 'anti-Semitic action, because M&S is a Jewish company' (untrue) and encouraged people to boycott the campaign. It was in fact the PSC which first weaponised allegations of anti-Semitism, not the right wing of the Labour Party.

For all their professed indignation at Zionist atrocities, the affinity of these opportunist forces to the Labour Party translated into efforts to control the Palestine solidarity movement and undermine those who opposed not just Israel, but British imperialism and its Labour cronies. Despite the grassroots support for the Second Intifada, the leadership of these opportunists frittered away the potential of that period.

Yet despite this, the Second Intifada remains one of the most important periods in the history of Palestinian resistance and solidarity both in Palestine and on the streets of Britain. As Palestinian journalist Ramzy Baroud wrote in regards to the Israeli repression of that period: 'Onslaughts that were designed to ravage and destroy a land and its people were in fact creating unity and igniting an awakening among the forces of good all over the world.' We must apply the lessons of that period as we build the movements that will carry on the legacy of the Intifada today.

chapter six

WHY IS SOLIDARITY WITH PALESTINE UNDER ATTACK?

▼ by *Wesam Khaled*
from *a speech to a London public meeting*
21 September 2018

We are here because of the recent attempts to silence critics of Israel by conflating their criticisms with anti-Semitism. The International Holocaust Remembrance Alliance definition, the vehicle by which this conflation is being made, includes a number of examples which are clearly aimed at delegitimising legitimate criticisms of the Israeli state. One particularly problematic example claims that it is anti-Semitic to say that 'the existence of a State of Israel is a racist endeavour'. In light of this, the first part of my talk will challenge this example directly, looking at the history of the establishment of the state of Israel and explaining why we stand by the statement that Israel is a racist state. In the course of that discussion, I will touch on the role that British imperialism has played in supporting the establishment of Israel. Lastly, given recent events I will briefly discuss the history of the Labour Party's support for Zionism.

Israel's racist roots

When people accuse us of being anti-Semitic or anti-Jewish, our response is that of course we are neither of those things, we are instead anti-Zionist. But what is Zionism?

The Zionist ideology developed in late 19th century Europe against a backdrop of centuries of varying levels of persecution of Jewish minorities. It was a middle class movement which sought to build a 'Jewish nation'. While a number of different locations for this Jewish nation were debated (various proposals, including Uganda and Argentina, were made at various times) eventually it was basically agreed that it would be located in Palestine.

Of course, proposing a Jewish nation in Palestine doesn't appear to give a whole lot of regard to the indigenous Palestinians who were already living there. But not much regard has ever been given to any of the people living under the yoke of imperialism, and settler-colonial states had already been established in the United States, Canada, Australia, and elsewhere. (Of course, these had all been established through genocide and ethnic cleansing of their own). This issue would of course crop up later when it came to the actual establishment of the Israeli state.

Throughout the early decades, the Zionist movement remained quite marginal. But, as many of you will know, in 1917 the British state declared its support for Zionism with the Balfour Declaration, named after Lord Arthur Balfour who was Foreign Secretary at the time. Balfour himself was a pretty vile racist. He is quoted as once saying: 'We have to face the facts. Men are not born equal, the white and black races are not born with equal capacities: they are born with different capacities which education cannot and will not change.' So, this is the sort of character we are dealing with in Balfour.

The precise wording of the Balfour Declaration was:

'His Majesty's government view with favour the establishment in Palestine of a national home for the Jewish people, and will use their best endeavours to facilitate the achievement of this object, it being clearly understood that nothing shall be done which may prejudice the civil and religious rights of existing non-Jewish communities in Palestine, or the rights and political status enjoyed by Jews in any other country.'

That middle bit about not prejudicing the rights of the non-Jewish communities living there sounds all well and good, but it was clear that this wasn't on Balfour's list of priorities. He later said: 'In Palestine we do not propose even to go through the form of consulting the wishes of the present inhabitants of the country... Zionism is rooted in age-long traditions, in present needs, in future hopes, of far profounder import than the desires of the 700,000 Arabs who now inhabit that ancient land.' As history would show, the rights of non-Jews in Palestine would not be a priority for the Zionists either.

In fact, even in relation to the last bit of the Declaration about protecting the rights and status of Jews in other countries there are reasons to believe Balfour was less than genuine. Balfour was quite anti-Semitic himself (as might be expected of a racist): in 1919 he wrote that the Zionist movement would 'mitigate the age-long miseries created for Western civilization by the presence in its midst of a Body which it too long regarded as alien and even hostile, but which it was equally unable to expel or to absorb.' Essentially he was saying Zionism would solve the problem of Jews living in Europe by exporting them to Palestine.

Such was Lord Balfour. But there were other reasons for British imperialism to support Zionism besides such anti-Semitic sentiments. In the words of Ronald Storrs, who became military governor of Jerusalem in the same year as the Balfour Declaration, the Zionist movement would create a 'little loyal Jewish Ulster in a sea of potentially hostile Arabism.' In other words, Israel would be a useful ally to British imperialist interests in the Middle East. The vital support offered by Israel to British and other imperialist intervention in the Middle East is evidence enough of this fact.

The British state also believed that by supporting Zionism it could counteract the influence of Bolshevism. Of course, traditional anti-Semitic tropes about communism being a global Jewish conspiracy were a significant factor in this thinking. In 1917, before the Bolshevik Revolution and Russia's withdrawal from the First World War, Britain thought that by supporting Zionism and sending a Zionist delegation to Russia it could counteract 'Jewish pacifist propaganda in Russia', thereby keeping its Russian ally in the war. In 1920, Winston Churchill wrote a document called 'Zionism vs Bolshevism' – filled with quite a bit of anti-Semitic imagery of its own – where he basically said that there were good

15 August 2022, Emergency Rally for Palestine, Manchester.

Jews and bad Jews, the good Jews being Zionists and the bad Jews being the Bolsheviks, and that Zionism must be supported so as to prevent Jews from being swayed to the international Jewish-communist conspiracy. So much for the greatest Briton.

In any case, Britain took control of Palestine after WWI after Britain and France carved up the defeated Ottoman Empire amongst themselves. With that and the Balfour Declaration, the Zionist movement found itself in a situation where the government in control of Palestine had declared its support for the establishment of a Jewish state there. Over the following decades hundreds of thousands of Jews would be encouraged to migrate to Palestine with varying degrees of British support. But the numbers migrating were insufficient to create a Jewish majority in the land of historic Palestine.

The core dilemma that Zionism continued to face was the question of how to create a Jewish-majority state in a land that was already inhabited overwhelmingly by non-Jews. Various strategies were devised to get rid of the Palestinians living there. One such strategy was to purchase as much land as possible for Jewish-only use. The Jewish National Fund

(JNF) was established in 1901 to buy up Palestinian land which could only be leased to Jews. Many Palestinian peasants found themselves evicted from their lands by Zionists who had bought it from its previous large landowners. Another strategy was discrimination in employment: Histadrut, the unified Zionist trade union in Palestine, enforced a racist policy of exclusively Jewish employment. But these tactics could only go so far. By 1947, when the UN introduced its Partition Plan, only 33% of the population of Palestine was Jewish.

Despite this, the UN Partition Plan, which proposed to separate Palestine into a Jewish and an Arab state, gave 55% of the land of Palestine to the Jewish state, leaving 45% for the majority Arabs. This was a massive victory and a step forward for the Zionist movement, but even that did not resolve the underlying problem. As David Ben-Gurion, who would become Israel's first Prime Minister, would lament later that year:

'In the area allocated to the Jewish State there are not more than 520,000 Jews and about 350,000 non-Jews, mostly Arabs... the total population of the Jewish State at the time of its establishment will be about one million, including almost 40% non-Jews. Such a composition does not provide a stable basis for a Jewish State. This fact must be viewed in all its clarity and acuteness. With such a composition, there cannot even be absolute certainty that control will remain in the hands of the Jewish majority ... There can be no stable and strong Jewish state so long as it has a Jewish majority of only 60%.'

As the prospect of realising a Jewish state in Palestine drew closer, Zionist leaders increasingly came to see the need to remove the Arabs from the land in one way or another. As Joseph Weitz, Director of the JNF, put it: 'It must be clear that there is no room in the country for both peoples ... The only solution is a Land of Israel ... without Arabs. There is no room here for compromises ...There is no way but to transfer the Arabs from here to the neighbouring countries, and to transfer all of them, save perhaps a few.' 'Transfer' is a very nice word to be using here. One might argue that 'ethnic cleansing' would be an appropriate substitute.

With the establishment of Israel in 1948 this transfer was finally put into action, forcibly and on a mass scale. Israeli militias and military forces attacked Palestinian towns and villages en masse between 1947 and 1949, killing 15,000 Palestinians. The most well-known instance was in the Palestinian village of Deir Yassin, where over 100 civilians were massacred in one day. Some of these were reported to have been mutilated, raped, and paraded through Jewish neighbourhoods before being executed. There are many more accounts of the atrocities of that period which I do not have time to go into here. I would recommend the book by Israeli historian Ilan Pappe, *The Ethnic Cleansing of Palestine*, for a more thorough account. All in all, between 1947 and 1948 around 850,000 Palestinians had been expelled from what is now the state of Israel, out of a total population of about 1.4 million. Over 500 Palestinian towns and villages were completely wiped off the map.

Out of this mass ethnic cleansing the solution to the dilemma of Israel's demographic balance had been found. By the end of this period Israel controlled 77% of historic Palestine, with a sizeable Jewish majorit

To this day, Israel continues to refuse the right of Palestinians who were expelled in that and later wars their right to return to their homeland. Palestinians who were born in the land, many of whom still hold the deeds to the land and the keys they used to open their homes, are not allowed to return. By contrast, any Jewish person in the world is allowed to apply to migrate to Israel under Israeli 'right to return' laws purely by virtue of their being Jewish.

The reasoning behind this racist exclusion is the same dilemma that has always plagued Zionism: what is sometimes referred to as the 'demographic threat' – the need to maintain a Jewish demographic majority.

All sorts of examples of racism can be seen cropping up throughout Israeli society and Israeli policy:

- A series of laws and practices that discriminate against Palestinian land ownership, including regular demolitions of Palestinian homes and discrimination against Palestinian building permit applications;
- The forced sterilisation by the Israeli state of Ethiopian Jews who

migrated to Israel (not only Palestinians suffer from the effects of the inherently racist character of the Israeli state);

- The recent much-maligned Nation State Law which effectively codifies the second-class citizen status of Arabs in Israel.

But these are really just symptoms of the fundamental underlying problem, the core contradiction of Zionism: the impossibility of maintaining a 'Jewish state' in Palestine, a land populated predominantly by non-Jews, without overwhelming violence and oppression. The need to avoid this 'demographic threat', this 'ethnic calculus' required to maintain a Jewish majority has been the driving force behind Zionist and Israeli policy towards the Palestinians from the very beginning. In the years before the state of Israel was established, it meant encouraging mass migration of Jews into Palestine. In 1948, it meant the forcible expulsion of the majority of Palestinians and the destruction of their villages. Today, it means continuing to deny the right of return to Palestinian refugees and refusing to grant political rights to the Palestinians living under Israeli occupation. The main reason why Israel hasn't tried to officially annex the West Bank yet is because of the unfavourable ethnic balance that would create. To grant citizenship to all of the Palestinians living

19 November 2023, Stop the bombing of Gaza demonstration, Glasgow

23 May 2021, Emergency Rally for Palestine, Birmingham.

in historic Palestine would immediately shrink the Jewish majority in Israel. Given Palestinian birth rates, it is estimated that the Palestinian population would become the majority in a few years. And that's the say nothing of the millions of Palestinian refugees living in exile. The result is what many have accurately called apartheid – millions of Palestinians living under Israeli occupation and effective Israeli control, but denied political and democratic rights. And of course, the massive settlement expansion into the occupied territories is another facet of the core issue, as Israel rapidly tries to establish a more favourable demographic make-up in as much Palestinian territory as possible.

All of these things are various forms of expressing that underlying contradiction, the need to maintain a Jewish majority. So tangible is this fear of ethnic imbalance that it even extends to particular regions of the Israeli state. In 2010, 1,300 armed Israeli police officers entered al-Araqib, a small impoverish Bedouin Palestinian village in the Negev desert, in southern Israel. They forcibly removed residents from their homes and destroyed 45 homes, leaving over 300 people homeless, half of whom were children. Two days earlier, Israeli Prime Minister Benjamin Netanyahu told government colleagues that a Negev 'without a Jewish majority' would pose a 'palpable' threat to the state. Such demolitions of Palestinian villages in the Negev are commonplace; Al-Araqib has been demolished and rebuilt over 130 times.

And the thing is, when Zionist leaders like Netanyahu and Ben-Gurion talk about Palestinian people and Palestinian towns posing an 'existential threat' to the state of Israel, they are absolutely correct! Let me be clear: I don't mean that Palestinians pose an existential threat to the lives of Jewish people in Israel, their safety or their security. What I mean is that insofar as Israel is to be characterised as a Jewish state, the Palestinian people will always pose a threat to it by the fact of their very existence, and the risk that they may ever exist in large enough numbers or concentrations to threaten Israel's ethnic composition. The right of Palestinians in the diaspora to return, the political rights of Palestinians in the occupied territories to full democratic rights – in short, the rights of the Palestinian people – do pose an existential threat to Israel.

This is what we mean when we say that Zionism is a racist ideology and that Israel is an inherently racist state. In addition to being founded on a racist settler-colonial mentality that gave no regard to the rights of the Palestinians, the actual realisation of Zionism's aims necessitated the destruction of the Palestinian nation. Israel's very existence as 'Israel', as a Zionist state, is premised on the denial of the fundamental rights of the Palestinians. It could not have been any other way.

To equate these criticisms of Zionism, Israel, or the foundation of the Israeli state with anti-Semitism is misguided at best and a deliberate attempt to undermine the just demands of the Palestinian people at worst.

The subjugation and expulsion of the Palestinian people, the denial of their rights to return and the enforcement of an apartheid system in Palestine, is not a coincidence, is not merely an avoidable consequence of bad policy or a few bad apples in an otherwise acceptable Zionist movement. Comrades, supporters, friends, we must be unequivocal in saying it: the destruction of the Palestinian nation and the oppression of the Palestinian people was and is a necessary precursor to the realisation of the Zionist goal, is an unavoidable consequence of the establishment and maintenance of the Israeli state. This is the core of the conflict in Palestine, and there will be no just resolution to that conflict without a struggle against its racist core. We are not anti-Semites. We are anti-Zionists.

chapter seven

CORBYN CAPITULATES TO ZIONISM

by *Robert Clough*
from *FRFI No.297*, September 2018

Jeremy Corbyn's capitulation in the face of a stream of spurious allegations of anti-Semitism is a complete betrayal of the Palestinian people. Faced with the choice of continuing the Labour Party's historic support for Zionism, or siding with an oppressed people fighting for their survival, Corbyn chose the former. His craven performance demonstrates that he lacks any principles. In the lead-up to the National Executive Committee (NEC) meeting on 4 September which adopted the full International Holocaust Remembrance Association (IHRA) definition of anti-Semitism, Palestinian Knesset members and civil organisations correctly described this definition as Zionist and urged Labour to reject it. But the Zionist bigots who demanded that Labour adopt the IHRA definition have nothing but contempt for the Palestinian people – and, in the end, so did Corbyn and his supporters. In order to retain his position as leader of a party completely wedded to imperialism, he has opened the gate for a renewed drive to criminalise and suppress Palestinian solidarity.

As part of the Zionist campaign, the media trawled through Corbyn's record to 'prove' his anti-Semitism; columnists in *The Guardian* were given free rein to attack him. Among the most ludicrous allegations were that:

- According to *The Times*, he had laid a wreath on the grave of a supposed leader of the 1972 Munich Olympics massacre when he visited Tunisia in 2014. This turned out to be a complete fiction: the wreath was laid on the graves of Palestinian victims of a 1985 Israeli airstrike which was denounced by the UN at the time as a war crime.

- He had stated in a meeting on Palestine in 2013 that the Zionists in the audience did not understand English irony, which led arch-Zionist MP Luciana Berger to complain that she now felt 'unwelcome in my own party', and former Chief Rabbi Jonathan Sacks to claim even more absurdly that Corbyn's comment was the most offensive since Enoch Powell's 1968 'rivers of blood' speech. Sacks supports Israel unconditionally and defends its racist Nation-State law. In 2008 he appeared in a list of 100 top right-wingers compiled by *The Daily Telegraph*, the only religious figure to appear in the list. Sacks' comparison of Powell's grossly racist speech to Corbyn's comment betrays his utter contempt for black and Asian people.

However, this reactionary campaign could have been stopped from the outset had Corbyn stood his ground. All he had to do was to demonstrate the utterly reactionary character of his opponents by pointing to any number of Israeli war crimes: the continuous ethnic cleansing of Palestinians from the West Bank and East Jerusalem; the situation of Palestinians in the open prison of Gaza, now blockaded for more than ten years; the 14 May massacre of more than 60 protesters demanding the right of return for Palestinian refugees; the use of checkpoints and the apartheid wall on the West Bank to ghettoise Palestinian people; the treatment of Palestinian child prisoners like Ahed Tamimi; the passage of the Nation-State law in July enshrining the racist character of the Zionist state. None of which have been criticised by Corbyn's racist critics. Yet he refused to do so. Instead he made repeated concessions to his Zionist opponents:

- In a leadership election debate in September 2016 organised by the Labour Friends of Israel (LFI) and Jewish Labour Movement (JLM), Corbyn stated that 'I admire the verve and spirit of the towns and cities in Israel. I admire the separation of legal and political powers in the system of democratic government that's there.' He did not mention the racism that governs the lives of Palestinian people living in Israel, nor as part of this, the state policy of denying Palestinian towns and villages meaningful funding.

- When Shadow Development Minister Kate Osamor declared her support for the boycott, divestment and sanctions (BDS) campaign in December 2017, a spokesperson for Corbyn stated 'Jeremy is not in favour of a comprehensive or blanket boycott. He doesn't support BDS,' adding that 'he would have no qualms with buying Israeli products himself.'

- He issued an abject apology for chairing a House of Commons meeting in 2010 saying that he has 'on occasion appeared on platforms with people whose views I completely reject.' Once again he made no reference to Palestinian oppression or Israeli terrorism. At the meeting Holocaust survivor Haja Meyer had denounced the Zionist use of the 'Nazi genocide of Jews to justify the ethnic cleansing of Palestine by the state of Israel' – this the Zionists decided was anti-Semitic even though it is historically accurate.

- He took no action against the millionaire reactionary MP Margaret Hodge when she shouted to his face that he was a 'fucking anti-Semite and racist'. Hodge, who led the vote of no confidence in 2016 against Corbyn, is now stepping up the campaign to drive him from the leadership.

- In an article he wrote for *The Guardian* (3 August 2018) Corbyn argued that the 'essence' of the four examples excluded from the IHRA definition had been captured in the Labour Party code of conduct, and that the actual differences 'are in fact very small'. 'All of us committed to peace and justice in the Middle East accept that the perspective of the Palestinian people, and their experience as victims of racism and discrimination, should not be censored or penalised any more than the right of Jewish self-determination should be denied.' Not a word about the fact that the exercise of that 'right' required the violent expulsion of 750,000 Palestinian people, or their continued experience of torture, murder and ethnic cleansing.

Throughout his *Guardian* article Corbyn is at pains to appease his enemies: he declares that 'In the 1970s some on the left mistakenly argued that "Zionism is racism". That was wrong.' This was an extraordinary statement: the United Nations General Assembly itself declared in 1975 that Zionism is a racist ideology, until in 1991 following the collapse of the socialist bloc, the US was able to garner sufficient support to overturn the resolution. That Zionism is racism is a fact, not a matter of opinion. Corbyn's language is like cotton wool: he characterises the passage of the Nation-State law and the murder of hundreds of unarmed Palestinian demonstrators (in Corbyn's non-judgemental language, 'killings') as 'a difficult year in the Middle East'. His repeated desire for a gentler political language is designed to dull the perception of his followers over the appalling brutality of the Zionist state. It took an attack from Israeli Prime Minister Benjamin Netanyahu for Corbyn to show any courage and condemn the May 2018 Israeli massacre of Palestinian demonstrators in Gaza.

In his written submission to the 4 September NEC debate, Corbyn claimed that adoption of the IHRA definition with all examples 'does not undermine freedom of expression on the Israel-Palestine conflict' – a stupid lie because it is used by universities in Britain and the US in

19 March 2022, March Against Racism, Central London

attempts to suppress pro-Palestine events, particularly the annual Israel Apartheid Week. His further statement that Zionism has had 'honourable proponents' in the Labour Party was just a wretched sop to its most reactionary wing. There was no acknowledgment of the opposition from the Palestinian Knesset MPs whose letter to *The Guardian* said the IHRA definition 'goes far beyond anti-Jewish animus to include anti-Zionism'. Palestinian civil organisations declared that the IHRA definition 'attempts to erase Palestinian history, demonise solidarity with the Palestinian struggle for freedom, justice and equality, suppress freedom of expression, and shield Israel's far-right regime of occupation, settler-colonialism and apartheid from effective measures of accountability in accordance to international law.' On the day of the NEC meeting, the Israeli Supreme Court approved the demolition of the Bedouin village of Khan Al Ahmar. Khan Al Ahmar is in Area C, an Israeli designation assigned to about 60% of the occupied West Bank which places it under exclusive Israeli control: the destruction of the village is to enable the construction of a motorway linking Zionist settlements.

In the days before the NEC vote there had been growing concern among liberals and supporters of Palestinian liberation at Corbyn's conciliation and obfuscation. Having stated that 'Jeremy Corbyn has no need to apologise for being the first Labour leader to oppose Zionism on moral grounds,' Ahmad Khalldi in *The Guardian* lamented that Corbyn 'has singularly failed to make the case in his own defence. Under a barrage of attacks on the anti-Semitism issue, he has retreated and backtracked, mumbled and fumbled as if he has something to hide, thereby undermining his credibility as leader and peacemaker alike' (29 August 2018). The radical journalist Jonathan Cook complains that 'Corbyn's allies in the Labour leadership have largely lost the stomach for battle' and that 'Corbyn himself has conceded too much ground on anti-Semitism ... He has tried to placate rather than defy the smearers. He has tried to maintain unity with people who have no interest in finding common ground with him. And as he has lost all sense of how to respond in good faith to allegations made in bad faith, he has begun committing

26 November 2023, Protest for Palestine, Liverpool

the cardinal sin of sounding and looking evasive – just as those who deployed the anti-Semitism charge hoped' (Counterpunch 24 August).

Yet Cook does miss a key point: Corbyn has to maintain unity with his enemies if the Labour Party is to remain a credible parliamentary body, and if he is to stand a chance of becoming prime minister. There are 70 Labour MPs affiliated to Labour Friends of Israel, and over 80% of all Labour MPs oppose Corbyn. He will not sacrifice this force on any matter of principle, and this ruled out any chance of him defending the rights of the Palestinian people: they became the victims of this British parliamentary charade.

Cook's insights are not shared by the British opportunist left. Within the Labour Party, the supposed radical Owen Jones opposes BDS, and spoke at a JLM conference in April 2017 to share his view that there indeed was a crisis of anti-Semitism in the Labour Party. BDS is endorsed by all Palestinian civic organisations. Given the JLM's links with the Israeli embassy, to speak on its platform was a gesture of contempt for the Palestinian people. Momentum leader Jon Lansman is a closet Zionist who regards Zionism as an 'outdated' term. Like Jones, he opposes BDS, having visited Tel Aviv in June to speak about the anti-Semitism 'problem' in the Labour Party. He supported the adoption of the full IHRA definition and, days beforehand, spoke at a JLM meeting at which he suggested that Corbyn should undertake an awareness course on anti-Semitism. There has been no reaction from Momentum: its silence on Lansman's position and behaviour can only be interpreted as indifference to the question of Palestinian solidarity – indeed, its members on the NEC voted in support of the IHRA definition.

Concerned that their hope for a Corbyn-led Labour government was slipping away, others on the left came out, not to build effective solidarity with the Palestinian people, but to worry about saving their own hides. Flying in the face of facts, Tariq Ali declared at a meeting organised by Jewish Voice for Labour (JVL) on 22 August that 'On Palestine, Corbyn has been rock-solid. That's why his opponents in and out of the Labour Party fear him.' Labour NEC candidate Huda Elmi added to the fiction by declaring that 'One of the things we have to be proudest about in the Labour movement is that we've stood consistently shoulder to shoulder with the Palestinians.' This is just fantasy: Labour has never supported the Palestinian people. Without mentioning names, SWP's Rob Ferguson declared that 'It has been a fundamental misjudgement over more than two years to retreat and concede and fail to call out those prosecuting this attack.' This is the SWP which showed itself to be very willing to 'retreat and concede' to Zionism when it fought to include a contingent of Zionists on a Stand up to Racism demonstration in Glasgow on 17 March this year. JVL's Richard Kuper said that if the fight against Labour's adoption of the full IHRA definition is lost, 'the war is not over' – citing the possibility of opposing councils adopting the definition. Yet Labour-led councils like Newcastle are falling over themselves to adopt the definition (if they have not already done so), with the Palestine Solidarity Campaign refusing to challenge them and Corbyn-supporting councillors running away to avoid being whipped into support.

Perhaps the most absurd comment came from Tony Greenstein who faced expulsion over a false allegation of anti-Semitism. Responding to an article on *Electronic Intifada* by Stephen Garside who said correctly that 'Tragically, the fight over the IHRA now looks to have also become a fight against Corbyn', Greenstein wrote that it was a very good article but for that phrase, continuing 'No we are not fighting against Corbyn but we will disagree with him when he backslides. That is very important. The whole of the false anti-Semitism campaign has one purpose in mind – removing Jeremy Corbyn. We must be very clear that we defend Jeremy's position even if he is unable to do so.' (emphasis added). What a comment about the leader of an imperialist party!

But the more Corbyn backslides, the more will be the desperation of the opportunist left to protect him and the Labour Party. Honest socialists now have to take stock. Corbyn was content to remain a Labour MP while Labour governments waged war in Yugoslavia and in the Middle East and excused every act of Israeli aggression. His opposition was always confined to meaningless parliamentary gestures, his supposed principles a myth. He capitulated to the Zionists when a principled stand would have swatted away the clearly reactionary campaign, given the daily displays of the racist character of the Israeli state. He leads a reactionary, anti-working class party. How can anyone other than a dyed-in-the-wool opportunist believe he has the willingness to withstand the slightest pressure if he leads a Labour government? As it is, he has demonstrated utter contempt for the position and views of the Palestinian people, and from now on the fight to build a solidarity movement will be a fight against Corbyn and his Labour Party.

20 January 2024, Protest for Palestine, Birmingham

chapter eight

HAMAS WINS PALESTINIAN ELECTIONS
No to Occupation!

▼ by *Bob Shepherd*
from *FRFI No.188*, December 2005/January 2006

Hamas's landslide victory in the elections to the Palestine Legislative Council (PLC) is, as Hamas political leader Mahmoud Zahar put it, 'a big slap to the Americans and Israelis'. With Fatah rapidly dissolving into warring factions and Ariel Sharon's stroke leaving the Zionists effectively leaderless, Bush's roadmap is now hopelessly discredited. All that imperialism can do for the moment is threaten to starve the Palestinian people into submission by withholding aid until Hamas abandons the armed struggle and recognises Israel.

In electing Hamas the Palestinian people have shown that despite more than five years of terror that have accompanied the latest Intifada, they remain unbowed. Their defiance, their refusal to roll over and do imperialism's bidding, has rocked imperialism back on its heels. It was not just a vote against the corruption of Fatah and the Palestinian Authority (PA) – it was a resounding vote against occupation. Despite the daily terror of the Israeli occupation, and their almost complete international isolation, the Palestinian people showed they will not give up their national aspirations and kneel down to the interests of Zionism and imperialism. They have delivered a major blow to imperialism as its strategy in the Middle East continues to unravel.

Both Bush and Blair were staggered at the scale of Hamas's victory. Blair stated that Hamas must decide 'between a path of democracy or a path of violence' while Bush argued cynically that 'if your platform is the destruction of Israel it means you're not a partner in peace, and we're interested in peace'. Mahmoud Zahar clearly answered their hypocrisy: 'We are under occupation. The Israelis continue aggression against our people; killing, detentions, demolitions. In order to stop this we are entitled to self-defence by all means including using guns. If the Israelis stop their aggression, we will be committed to the calm-down'.

Election results

In all Hamas won 76 out of 132 seats on the Legislative Council: 46 out of 66 directly elected regional seats as against Fatah's 16, and 30 out of 66 distributed according to the votes won by national lists. Fatah ended up with a mere 43 seats in all. The call by Islamic Jihad for a boycott of the election did not seriously affect the turnout, which was estimated to be about 74%.

Imperialist commentators have tried to present the result as merely a no confidence vote in Fatah and PA corruption in order to minimise its significance. Hamas of course made these issues central in the election. But there was also Hamas's welfare record: its organisation of social welfare, schools, universities and hospitals especially in Gaza. Whilst Fatah and PA leaders creamed off millions of dollars of aid that flooded in after the 1993 Oslo peace agreement, the mass of the Palestinian people sank further into destitution. For many, Hamas's social programmes were what kept them from starvation. For hundreds of thousands of Palestinians, Fatah and PA corruption was clearly payment for services rendered to imperialism: aid had created a completely parasitic and dependent bourgeoisie whose only interest was to sell their national rights to imperialism.

The elections had gone ahead despite widespread calls for them to be postponed or abandoned. Such calls came not only from the imperialists and Zionists, but also from sections of the ruling Fatah movement, clearly worried at an early stage about the level of support they would command in the new PLC. In an act of naked intimidation, both the US and the EU threatened to suspend financial support for the PA if Hamas ended up in government. Israeli troops established at least 400 checkpoints and roadblocks in the run-up to the election and imposed severe restrictions on the movement of candidates throughout the West Bank and on Palestinian communities isolated between the 'Green Line' and the Apartheid Wall. Candidates were also banned from travelling between the West Bank and Gaza.

The Zionists also tried to undermine the legitimacy of the elections by threatening to prevent the quarter of a million Palestinians living in East Jerusalem from taking part. The response of Mahmoud Abbas was to suggest that if this happened then the elections should be cancelled. Hamas, whilst supporting the right of East Jerusalem Palestinians to vote, insisted that the election should go ahead regardless. As it was, on 15 January, just ten days before the elections were due to take place, the Israeli government agreed to allow limited campaigning in East Jerusalem, but banned any campaigning for election lists attached to resistance groups. This was of course a futile attempt to prevent Hamas gaining support. Candidates from both Hamas and the Popular Front for the Liberation of Palestine were arrested in East Jerusalem in the run-up to the election. The election procedure for citizens of East Jerusalem was to be the same as it was for the 2005 presidential election: they had to go to one of five post offices to cast their votes. The purpose of this exercise was to enable the Zionists to describe this as a postal vote since they do not recognise any Palestinian rights in Jerusalem.

Fatah – squabbling over the crumbs from imperialism

Fatah, which has dominated Palestinian politics since the end of the 1960s, was riven by division in the run-up to the election, principally between the 'old guard' associated with Oslo and Arafat, and the 'new guard' including the leadership of the Aqsa Martyrs Brigade (AMB) which has played a leading role in both the first and second Intifadas. The 'old guard', which had controlled the PA since its inception was determined to continue excluding the 'new guard' and retain its access to wealth and privilege.

Indicative of this were Fatah internal elections last November to agree their candidates. The 'old guard' largely ignored the results and placed itself at the head of the Fatah election list. This led in early December to a split in Fatah with rival election lists being presented. One, put forward by the 'new guard' and calling itself the Future Bloc, had Marwan Barghouti at its head, and included his wife and Mohammed Dahlan, the former PA Civil Affairs Minister. The official Fatah list put forward by Abbas also opportunistically had Barghouti at its head. The Future Bloc's inclusion of Dahlan, a millionaire widely accused of corruption, clearly showed that there was no fundamental class difference between the two sides, and that the dispute was solely over which set of individuals would get access to the PA's finances. Although Fatah eventually presented a unified list, in many places Fatah members who did not make the official lists stood as independents. The resultant split in the Fatah vote helped Hamas to its overwhelming victory, particularly in the regional seats.

The squabbles between the factions continued throughout the election campaign. Sections of AMB occupied offices of the Central Election Commission in Gaza calling for the elections to be cancelled, as their representatives had not been put on the national Fatah list. In the West Bank the AMB in Nablus threatened to disrupt and stop the voting: 'Neither the PA, Fatah, nor Hamas has done anything for the Palestinian people as we witness daily Israeli occupation forces incursions and assassinations, without anyone providing protection to the Palestinian people, so on what grounds are we holding the elections?' asked Ala Şanakra, leader of the AMB in Nablus.

Hamas's political strategy

For Hamas the elections provided an opportunity to follow up its success in the municipal election and gain a level of national representation that reflected its support on the ground.

Hamas is clearly evolving and it adapted its strategy and political programme to maximise its electoral chances. For instance, it suspended military attacks on Israel during the election period. All the rocket strikes on Israel from Gaza during this time were carried out by Islamic Jihad, AMB and the Popular Resistance Committees. This was a complete change from September when Hamas was in the forefront of such attacks. According to one Hamas candidate, 'the policy is to maintain the armed struggle but it is not our first priority. We know that first of all we have to put more effort into resolving the internal problems, dealing with corruption, blackmail, and chaos. This is our priority because if we change the situation for the Palestinians it will make our course stronger...Hamas is looking to establish a new political strategy, in which all Palestinian groups will participate, not just dominated by Fatah. We will discuss the negotiation strategy, how can we run the conflict with Israel but by different means.' (*The Guardian* 12 January)

Another Hamas candidate, Aziz Dweik, from the West Bank city of Al Khalil (Hebron), said Hamas had no choice but to moderate its political language: 'Eventually we will have to distinguish between the ideological and the political'. He added Hamas recognised the need to show 'political responsibility' and 'moderation' once it reached parliament. When it was clear that Hamas had an overwhelming victory Hamas leader Ismail Haniyeh told the BBC 'don't be afraid, Hamas is an aware and mature movement... which is politically open in the Palestinian...and the international arena.'

The future

Hamas and the Palestinian people are now under renewed pressure to 'win international acceptance' – that is, to capitulate. In imperialism's world, where aggressors become victims and victims aggressors, US, British and Israeli politicians queue up to condemn Hamas as terrorists whilst ignoring the root cause of the violence – Zionist occupation. The US intends to suspend $400m aid; EU foreign policy chief Javier Solana says that Europe will also halt hundreds of millions of dollars in aid unless Hamas recognises Israel's right to exist. With Abbas isolated and his Fatah organisation disintegrating, imperialism has lost the principal vehicle for representing its interests amongst the Palestinian people. That this has coincided with Sharon's incapacitation merely compounds its problems. As the Palestinian people stand against their persecutors, we need to intensify our solidarity work in this country.

REVIEW OF
chapter nine

THE HOLOCAUST INDUSTRY
reflections on the exploitation of Jewish suffering
by Norman G Finkelstein, Verso, 2000

by *Jackie Kaye*
from *FRFI No.157*, October/November 2000

In his tightly-argued book, *The Holocaust Industry: reflections on the exploitation of Jewish suffering,* Norman G Finkelstein makes three points: the true horror of the Nazi holocaust is lost in the inflation of the numbers of those who survived and the refusal to acknowledge non-Jewish victims; the compensation industry for the victims has been used to justify uncritical support for the state of Israel; huge sums of money remain in US banks under the control of wealthy and powerful Jewish groups.

Aficionados of detective fiction everywhere learn early that it is often the most obvious things which are the hardest to see. Finkelstein draws our attention to one such fact: at the end of World War II all authorities agreed that no more than 100,000 Jews had survived the concentration camps. Fifty years later, given average mortality rates, the number still alive would be around 25,000. Yet, according to those mounting claims for compensation, the number is said to be nearer one million. These survivors have not merely survived, they have gone forth and multiplied. They have achieved, it would appear, immortality.

The reasons for this are simply our old friends cash and carry. The more survivors, the more money that can be extorted on their behalf from anyone and everyone deemed 'guilty' by the self-appointed bodies running the compensation business which Finkelstein calls The Holocaust

Industry. This industry has created a fiction called The Holocaust which is quite distinct from the historical event which is the Nazi holocaust.

This capitalised Holocaust - and that pun is intentional - is the creation not of National Socialism but of the Jewish lobby in the United States. It tells us a great deal about the USA and nothing at all about what happened in Europe in the 1930s and 1940s. Here is a terrifying insight into the darkest heart of the capitalist adventure known as the American dream. It shows us how well-to-do, successful and highly integrated and compliant Jewish elites came to realise how they could make financial and moral capital out of the past sufferings of poor, European Jews and that these victims were not the embarrassing losers they appeared to be.

The turning point was the 1967 victory by Israel over the Arab countries in the Six Day War. Until then, Israel itself had been classed as a 'loser' state by Jewish elites who had seen it as dependent on US handouts. These same elites had disassociated themselves from the efforts by left-wing Jewish organisations to keep the record of fascism alive, supported McCarthyism and the death penalty for the Rosenbergs and claimed that Soviet anti-Semitism was worse than that of the Nazis. After the 1967 war Israel emerged as a hero nation and these elites wished to benefit from the US government's endorsement of Israel's strategic significance in the Middle East. In so doing, they have strengthened Zionist reaction, impeded a just settlement of the Palestinian conflict and turned Washington into 'Israeli-occupied territory'. But they have reaped benefits which can be regarded as moral and material capital. Firstly, they have achieved 'victim' status, a sine qua non of US ethnic politics. Secondly, they have created a vast extortion racket for milking funds from European banks, industries and individuals in the guise of compensation for the sufferings of Jewish slave labourers. This racket has not investigated money deposited in US and Israeli banks by Jews threatened by the Nazis, nor has any compensation money been paid to Jewish survivors living in Israel. It remains firmly in the control of US Jewish organisations. Indeed only 15% of the money collected has been paid to individual survivors. The rest has been siphoned off into the pockets of lawyers, rabbis, community projects and something called 'Holocaust education', of which the Imperial War Museum in London is the latest example.

The symbol of their achievement is the Washington Holocaust Memorial Museum. The Holocaust industry has made the Holocaust into a US memory. Right on the Mall in Washington, alongside the statues of Washington and Lincoln, museums dedicated to United States history, art, industry, and far more visible than the underground memorial to the Vietnam War, is a Holocaust experience for a nation who did not have that particular Holocaust. Notably absent from the Mall is any memorial or record of African slavery, the attempted genocide of the Native Americans or the Chinese slave labourers who died building the railways, let alone the hundreds of thousands of Africans, Latin Americans and Asians who were slaughtered in the rage of capitalist expansion disguised as the war against communism. The American Jewish elites reinvented themselves as 'victims', a necessary makeover in the nursery politics of the United States. The ruling classes in the States are allowed to disremember the real history of their nation and replace it with what Finkelstein calls the 'Dachau meets Disney' of the Holocaust experience. Everyone gets to make a lot of money.

Finkelstein points out that 17 states encourage or mandate the teaching of the Holocaust and that US public schools which lack books, writing materials and teachers are supplied with Holocaust literature at public expense. The Washington Holocaust Museum is funded with $30 million of public money. We too are threatened with a Holocaust holy day. None of this would be possible without the craven compliance of academia which has bought wholesale into the comforting fakery of memory and hastily jettisoned the discomforting challenges of power and commitment. Holocaust Chairs now proliferate and Holocaust denial becomes the sin without pardon. Deborah Lipstadt is the doyenne of Holocaust denial detection. Holocaust denial, absurd and repellent as it is, is given some credibility by Lipstadt's definition: to question a survivor's testimony, to denounce the role of Jewish collaborators, to suggest the Germans

suffered during the bombing of Dresden, or that any state except Germany
committed crime in World War II.

Israeli writer Boas Evron accurately notes that:

*'Holocaust awareness is an official, propagandistic indoctrination, a
churning out of slogans and a false view of the world, a real aim of
which is not at all an understanding of the past, but a manipulation of
the present.' (p41)*

In order to achieve this, Holocaust propagandists have to make two
manifestly false claims. One is that the Nazi holocaust was a unique event;
the second, that it represented the culmination of thousands of years of
irrational hatred of the Jews. These dogmas, of course, come very close
to the Nazis' own justification for the extermination of the Jews. They
both involve the concept of Jewish uniqueness. This is argued by pseudo-
scholars like Daniel Goldenhagen in his now discredited *Hitler's Willing
Executioners* as well as by neo-Nazis like David Irving. In his failed libel
action against Lipstadt, Irving asserted that Jews should look into their
mirrors each morning and ask 'Why does everyone hate me?'

Holocaust industry apologists claim that Jews are different because
everyone hates them. That's why they need their own states which must
be exempted from the laws which apply to all other nations because
Jews are not like anyone else. The sins of Zionism have been paid for in
advance by the blood of Auschwitz. That is also the reason why industry
spokesmen have been determined that no one else should be allowed to
muscle in on the act. Other victims of Nazi persecution such as gypsies,
communists and gays are rigorously excluded from the memory game. A
spokesman for the Washington Museum committee is quoted as saying
that the gypsies are not 'really a people'. Niemoller's famous quote has
been altered in the Museum so that the phrase 'When they came for the
Communists I did nothing' has been left out. Elie Wiesel refused to take
part in a conference on genocide held in Israel because it would have
included representatives of the Armenian victims of the Turkish state.
Wiesel, along with the American Jewish Committee, American Jewish
Congress, Bnai Brith and the Anti-defamation League have not only never

protested against Israeli onslaughts against Palestinians, they have sought to blame Palestinian leaders in the 1940s for the Nazi atrocities! Wiesel attacked Simon Peres for linking Auschwitz with Hiroshima. Holocaust industry spokesmen have not spoken out against genocide in Rwanda, the slaughter in East Timor, the use of Zyklon B gas by Saddam Hussein against the Kurds, to mention just three recent experiences where one might have expected that sheer human empathy might have carried some weight.

The false claim of Jewish uniqueness, mirroring the ideology of anti-Semites everywhere, is the bedrock of the Holocaust industry. It is also becoming a main fomenter of growth in anti-Semitism, especially in impoverished but newly-privatised Eastern Europe, where Holocaust industry claims for compensation are threatening to dispossess and further pauperise some of the most disadvantaged people in Europe. Claims there from Jews still living in the ex-Soviet bloc will only be met if they are adherents of a recognised religious practice. So this money will fund a `revival' of Judaism in these countries and undoubtedly many people will, like Madeleine Albright, wake up one day and remember that they are Jewish.

At the end of the day, this all comes down to numbers: bodies and dollars. Again a discomfiting parallel from the past comes to mind: the price per head the Nazis collected from Jews they allowed to leave. An Israeli newspaper, *The Jerusalem Report*, claimed on 15 June 1999, that the American Claims Conference, which now handles all compensation actions, `has plenty to gain by ensuring the survivors get nothing'. While Knesset member Michael Kleiner called the Conference 'A Judenrat carrying on the Nazis' work in different ways'. The numbers game of the Holocaust industry makes disturbing reading. Numbers of survivors have been boosted by strategies such as the inclusion of Polish Jews who spent the whole war in Russia; the relatives of those who survived the camps; Jews who spent the war hiding or in neutral countries; Jews who had no connection with the camps but who were traumatised by hearing about them; non-Jews who imaginatively empathised with the plight of the Jews and even those who wrote fake accounts are acclaimed and claimed by this multi-million dollar enterprise.

'In fact, to believe the Holocaust industry, more former Jewish slave labourers are alive today than half a century ago...In juggling these numbers the Holocaust industry...whitewashes Nazism. Raul Hilberg, the leading authority on the Nazi holocaust, puts the figure for Jews murdered at 5.1 million. Yet, if 135,000 former Jewish slave labourers are still alive today, some 600,000 must have survived the war. That's at least a half-million more than standard estimates. One would then have to deduct this half-million from the 5.1 million figure of those killed...the numbers of the Holocaust industry are rapidly approaching those of the Holocaust deniers.' (p127)

Does this kind of juggling with numbers make you feel uneasy? The idea that some kind of accounting can be used to compute the suffering inflicted at Auschwitz is abhorrent. Yet it is the basic fantasy of capitalism that everything has a price. When money interposes itself between the human and the real, we can never learn from history. Money cushions us against the horror of what we are capable of and comforts us with the delusion that there is no pain without a price that will make everything all right.

The Holocaust industry teaches us nothing about how we may safeguard our futures against such dark nights of the soul. We learn only what we knew already: the human greed for gold makes us less than human.

15 May 2022, Nakba Day protest, Nottingham

chapter ten

ISRAEL/PLO AGREEMENT AT OSLO
the great betrayal

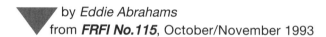 by *Eddie Abrahams*
from *FRFI No.115*, October/November 1993

The Declaration of Principles signed by the Israeli government and the Palestine Liberation Organisation on 13 September 1993 is a contemptuous and humiliating insult to all those who have died and all those who continue to fight for national and social liberation in Palestine.

The agreement proposes to establish a Palestinian Interim Self-Governing Authority (PISGA) across the whole of the Occupied Territories beginning with the poverty stricken and strategically insignificant Gaza Strip and the 100 square kilometres around Jericho city. A 'final settlement' is then scheduled within five years of the formation of the Self-Governing Authority. This 'peace'-plan is neither new nor radical. It is the fruit of the Madrid Peace Process begun in October 1992. What was evident then remains the case today:

'At the heart of this conflict is the right of the Palestinian people to form an independent state in Palestine. This right is rejected, even in principle, by the USA and Israel. How can one talk of a serious (peace) conference when Palestinian self-determination does not even feature on the agenda. All that is on offer is a 'transitional period' of 'autonomy' ... lasting some 3 to 5 years ... following which the promise of a final settlement. An old scheme, dismissed in 1988 by the then Palestinian mayor of Ramallah as 'power to collect garbage and exterminate mosquitoes'! Nevertheless, today, with the intifada beleaguered and

isolated, imperialism hopes that offering the Palestinian bourgeoisie the sop of 'autonomy' will be enough to silence the challenge of the intifada.' (FRFI 104, Dec 1991/ Jan 1992)
Less than one year later, the leadership of the PLO, headed by Yassir Arafat, has accepted the sop and abandoned all the national and democratic ideals of the Palestinian evolution. In exchange for what amounts to a neo-colonial, apartheid bantustan style 'autonomy', Arafat promises to try and terminate not just the intifada but the armed struggle and the Palestinian revolution itself. While Palestinian workers and peasants continue to suffer aggravated poverty and are gunned down in their own streets, Arafat committed the PLO to:

'encourage and call upon the Palestinian people in the West Bank and Gaza Strip to take part in steps leading to the normalisation of life...'
(Letter to Norwegian Foreign Minister, Financial Times, 10 September 1993)

In another letter to Israeli Prime Minister Yitzhak Rabin, equating the revolutionary armed struggle of the oppressed with violence and terrorism, Arafat states:

'... the PLO renounces the use of terrorism and other acts of violence and will assume responsibility over all PLO elements and personnel in order to assure their compliance, prevent violations and discipline violators.' (ibid)

It is hardly surprising that the PLO has now split, with the left-wing Popular Front for the Liberation of Palestine (PFLP) and the Democratic Front for the Liberation of Palestine (DFLP) resigning from the PLO executive along with a number of other opposition groups. George Habash, leader of the PFLP, has urged the Palestinian movement to hurl Arafat into the 'dustbin of history'. These forces are attempting to forge an alliance to organise and mobilise popular opposition to the deal.

This 'peace'-plan does nothing to advance even the most elementary requirements of the vast majority of Palestinians for popular power, self-determination and independent economic development. The response of the underground leadership of the intifada in the West Bank and Gaza

Strip makes the issues abundantly clear:

'The agreement reached between a branch of the PLO and the Zionist enemy does not meet the minimum demands that were raised by our masses when the uprising started. No Israeli withdrawal has been achieved, no recognition of the Palestinian national rights, no establishment of a Palestinian state and no freeze and removal of the settlements.'

The signing of the Declaration marks the final end to the PLO's role as a vanguard anti-Zionist, anti-imperialist movement in the Middle East. It represents a victory for Zionism, imperialism and the Arab bourgeoisie. Within the Palestinian arena it is a victory for the PLO's bourgeois trends and a defeat for the mass movement. The Palestinian bourgeoisie and their political representatives in the PLO are making their final peace with Zionism and imperialism. They are being willingly incorporated into a reactionary alliance against the working class, peasantry and poor of the entire region.

The 'peace'-plan for a bantustan

The neo-colonial, anti-working class, anti-popular character of the PLO-Israel agreement is hard to dispute. The PISGA, once it is established, will have no power whatsoever over Zionist settlements which include the richest and most fertile areas of the Occupied Territories.

It will have no jurisdiction over any Israeli citizens in any part of the Occupied Territories. It will have no authority over refugees or foreign affairs or relations with neighbouring countries. And it will have no control over Arab east Jerusalem. The Israeli police and army will have free use of all roads within the PISGA.

The PISGA itself will be a glorified local council with 'power' over health, welfare, education and tourism. It will also be required to form a Palestinian police force to keep law and order. This plan is but a modification of Israeli proposals advanced earlier this year:

'All land occupied by Zionist settlers, all roads, military zones and public land, including the Jordan Valley and the West Bank Highlands

will come under complete Israeli jurisdiction. This amounts to over 70 per cent of the Occupied Territories!
Palestinian autonomy over the remaining portions of land will be the autonomy of a bantustan. Israel will retain control of internal security and foreign relations. It will in addition control the infrastructure and water supplies, all land which is not privately owned and will have power to determine who shall or shall not reside in the Occupied Territories. These proposals merely transfer to Palestinians an existing colonial administration over which Israel will retain ultimate power through parallel structures of 'residual authority'. (FRFI 113, June/July 1993)

Even while signing the agreement, the Israeli government ploughs on remorselessly with its programme to complete 11,000 housing units constituting the largest ever building programme in the Occupied Territories. This is part of Rabin's plan to rationalise the expansion and development of Zionist settlements. Their strategic distribution and the network of roads and military zones linking them will secure Zionist control of the largest part of the Territories and restricts Palestinians to four enclaves in the West Bank, and two in Gaza, all isolated from each other and totally dependent on Israel.

Twenty six years of Israeli occupation have destroyed the economy of the West Bank and Gaza subordinating it totally to the needs of the Zionist settlers and Israeli capital. The combined Gross Domestic Product of the West Bank and Gaza is but 5 per cent of that of Israel. Gross National Product per head in the West Bank is just $2,000 while in the Gaza it is $1,200. The Israeli figure is $10,800. In this context it is downright treachery to speak of an independent Palestinian state even in the Occupied Territories as a whole, let alone in just the Gaza and Jericho. In the Gaza Strip at least 260,000 of the areas 780,000 people live in squalid refugee camps. Male unemployment now stands at 62 per cent and poverty is becoming desperate. An UNRWA official, Alex Pollock, notes that nearly all the area's infrastructure is 'either missing or in a deplorable state'.

This makes talk of the PISGA being merely a preparatory stage towards an independent Palestine, in a 'final settlement' five years hence, nothing but a deception. By then no Palestinian entity will exist! The Israeli government has repeatedly made clear, along with the US, its total opposition to any independent Palestinian state. Even as the 'peace'-deal was being signed in Washington, Israel issued a statement via its Paris embassy reiterating its 'opposition to the creation of an independent Palestinian state'.

The Declaration says nothing about the 'right of return' for Palestinians refugees expelled from their homeland from 1948 onwards. It leaves intact the entire Zionist colonial-settler state and military machine, ready to be used against resurgent revolutionary movements or other forces hostile to imperialism. Since the agreement President Clinton has assured Israel that there will be no cut in billions of dollars of US aid and military assistance.

Accord unites imperialist capital and the PLO against the people

The leaders of the USA, EC and Japan welcomed the Declaration as a decisive step to end the Palestinian revolution which over the decades presented the greatest threat to imperialist control over the region and its oil riches. They all understand however that the devastated economy of the Occupied Territories cannot sustain a stable bantustan PISGA. Poverty and desperation will breed opposition and threaten a revival of a revolutionary challenge. It is necessary therefore to take precautions. First they will try to bribe and silence this opposition. In the words of Alex Pollock:

'... a well-funded programme could immediately provide jobs, alleviate [he proposes merely to alleviate not eliminate] suffering and defeat political opposition.' (Financial Times, 10 September 1993)

An EC diplomat put the same message in a different way:

'Steps will have to be taken to support the population there otherwise the politics of despair will take over very quickly.' (The Guardian, 1 September 1993)

To this end imperialism is preparing a financial package with promises from the EC, the US, Japan and a number of Scandinavian countries. Meanwhile Arafat is touring the oil-rich Middle East governments begging for money to help buy support for the plan. Lest this bribery does not work, the Financial Times reminds us that the Declaration:

> *'commits the new Palestinian police force to co-operate with Israeli security forces in combating Hamas and other radicals in the territories which remain committed to the armed struggle.' (Financial Times, 15 September 1993)*

Abdullah Hourani, an independent member of the PLO Executive who has now resigned, quite correctly said:

> *'This agreement transforms the Palestinian autonomy authority into a repression apparatus against our people in favour of Israel.' (Financial Times, 13 September 1993)*

Large sections of Palestinians, even those among the ranks of Yassir Arafat's Al Fatah, see through the fraud of the Declaration. 180 Al Fatah guerrillas in Jordan issued a statement refusing to join the. proposed Palestinian police force:

> *'We are ready to serve in a nationalist police force in an independent Palestinian state, but not to be tools to suppress our peoples' resistance against the Israeli occupation.' (ibid)*

Who gains, who loses?

The only beneficiaries of the Declaration are the imperialists, the Zionists and the Arab/Palestinian bourgeoisie. The end of the Palestinian revolution will mean greater security for imperialist oil profits in the region. For the Zionists it opens the possibility of much more systematic and peaceful colonisation of Palestine (See FRFI 113, June/July 1993). The Declaration is a critical component of Zionism's strategy:

> *'By incorporating the Arab states into a settlement with Zionism, it isolates the Palestinian national liberation struggle. By seeking to incorporate the Palestinian bourgeoisie into an effectively colonial settlement, the Israeli state is then left free to turn against the Palestinian masses — the working class, the peasantry, the poor —*

who have nothing to gain from the process, not even an independent
Palestine.' (FRFI 113, June/July 1993)
These accords will enable Israel to rapidly sign agreements with
surrounding Arab regimes and end the regional blockade against them.
Israel then expects to emerge as a dominant economic force in the area.
Already Israeli economists are talking of 'major opportunities in terms
of export markets and imports of natural resources' and expecting a 22%
increase in exports.

As for the Arab and Palestinian bourgeoisie — well they can grovel
for crumbs from imperialism without having to concern themselves
about the wrath of the poor and oppressed. With the termination of the
Palestinian revolution, the Palestinian bourgeoisie, with financial help
from imperialist and Arab capital, hopes to carve itself a little niche as
a subordinate partner of Zionism and Arab reaction. Preparing to enter
the imperialist fold, the Palestinian bourgeoisie is eager to reassure
imperialism that the PLO will abandon all ambitions for an economically
independent and socially just Palestine. Hisham Awartani, a bourgeois
Palestinian economics professor, according to the *Financial Times*, is
urging the PLO to:

'recast itself to face the challenge: first it must resist socialist voices
calling for a state controlled economy and nationalist voices demanding
economic isolation from Israel.' (10 September 1993)
Awartani is forthright about the need of the PLO to remove itself from
the influence of 'trade unions, labour groups and old-time socialists.' The
PLO must, in other words oppose these groups' demands for social and
economic justice — demands which represent the interests of the vast
majority of Palestinians.

The PLO, the Palestinian bourgeoisie and the Revolution

The fundamental issue that today confronts socialists and anti-imperialists
is to explain why and how the PLO, once a powerful symbol of anti-
imperialist struggle, has surrendered with such a whimper. Why has

25 June 2023, protest outside the Israeli Embassy in London.

it signed a 'peace'-accord which, in the words of Ali Jiddah, a PFLP supporter who spent 17 years in a Zionist prison (interviewed in FRFI 101 June/July 1991), 'is a total subjection of the Palestinians to Israeli and American conditions.'

Current developments are the culmination of a long process spanning some two and a half decades during which the right-wing, bourgeois and petit-bourgeois trends within the PLO, represented primarily by Al-Fatah, have sought to seize total control of the organisation and curtail and stifle the truly popular, anti-imperialist, anti-capitalist struggle of the Palestinian masses.

During 26 years of the Zionist occupation and economic subjugation of the West Bank and Gaza Strip, the Palestinian bourgeoisie and wealthier sections of the petit-bourgeoisie became internally integrated into the Zionist economy. Externally they were also dependent on the flow of aid from the oil-rich pro-imperialist Gulf states. Within the Arab diaspora, the substantially wealthy Palestinian bourgeoisie has always tied its fortunes to the bourgeoisie of the Arab world rather than the popular democratic struggle of the masses. As a result, the Palestinian right-wing's commitment to the national liberation struggle has always been qualified by its own narrow class interests and by its ties to the Arab bourgeoisie and the Zionist economy. Its interests are therefore opposed to a consistent and uncompromising struggle against Zionism, imperialism or capitalism.

The Palestinian bourgeoisie saw the national struggle as no more than a stepping stone to greater profits unfettered by Zionist rule. It opposed Israel's occupation of the West Bank and Gaza because the occupation curtailed its own economic advancement, not because it devastated the lives of the masses. For the Palestinian bourgeoisie, the mass popular revolution was but a bargaining counter to be used in its selfish dealings with imperialism and Zionism. Like the bourgeois trend in all other liberation movements, the right wing of the PLO could not express or fight for the needs of the majority. Quite the contrary, it has always opposed the popular, socialist and revolutionary nationalist trends within the PLO.

At the peak of the PLO's anti-imperialist role, these left-wing and revolutionary nationalist trends were serious contenders to take over the leadership of the struggle. Imperialism therefore, in alliance with Zionism and the Arab bourgeoisie, spared no violence to destroy them. In September 1970, King Hussein's army suppressed a mass insurrection and drove the PLO out of Jordan. In 1976 Assad's Syrian regime used its army to save the Lebanese fascist falange from defeat at the hands of a joint democratic and leftist Lebanese/Palestinian alliance. Again in 1982, the PLO was subjected to savage attack when Israel invaded Lebanon killing 25,000 people. In 1984, the Syrian regime again intervened to stifle a resurgent left-wing popular alliance. From 1988 onwards the imperialists and Arab regimes ensured the total isolation of the intifada. This facilitated the Zionist repression which worked to drain and exhaust a mass popular movement which was moving to establish popular power and dual power.

These repeated assaults severely weakened the position of the left and revolutionary nationalist forces. They allowed the bourgeois forces to consolidate their position within the PLO which underwent a process of degeneration. Gulf oil money helped to nurture a privileged anti-democratic, bureaucratic stratum whose comfortable existence decisively separated it off from the lives and experience of the majority of the Palestinian poor and exploited. Thus the Palestinian bourgeoisie and its political representatives in the PLO lost any semblance of political principle and political independence. They steadily moved to tie their fortunes more tightly to the Arab ruling class. They abandoned the revolutionary and armed struggle and in return hoped that imperialism would reward them by pressurising Zionism into a compromise settlement.

The Gulf War marked a crucial turning point for these forces. The Arab ruling classes' willing alliance with the US in its war to crush Iraq, marked the Arab bourgeoisie's total submission to imperialism and the final humiliation and disintegration of the Arab nationalist movement. This totally isolated the Palestinian bourgeoisie, especially after the PLO, due to mass Palestinian anti-imperialist sentiment, was forced to support Iraq during the War. With an end to Gulf oil funding and with support from the Arab world at its lowest level, the PLO also faced a major political and financial crisis. Meanwhile on the West Bank and Gaza accelerated Zionist colonisation was threatening the remaining Palestinian bourgeois privileges. In these conditions, the PLO's bourgeois leadership threw in the towel and prepared to sue for peace on any conditions. They got the Madrid Conference and now the Declaration of Principles.

In its cowardly compromising behaviour the Palestinian bourgeoisie reflects in a concentrated form the character of the Arab bourgeoisie and indeed the bourgeoisie of most oppressed nations in the post-Soviet, new colonial times. Today they have abandoned all programmes for genuine independent national development and are prostrating themselves before their imperialist masters. The Arab ruling class was willingly incorporated into the imperialist alliance to crush Iraq. In the Third World as a whole, the ruling class has enthusiastically endorsed neo-liberalism which is enabling imperialism to once again seize total control of the world's natural resources and labour.

During the great anti-colonial and anti-imperialist struggles of the post-war period things were different. The strength and economic performance of the USSR stood as an example of the possibilities, even to the vacillating bourgeois and petit-bourgeois trends, of independent economic development. The existence of the Soviet Union was a fetter on imperialism and offered the anti-colonial and anti-imperialist movements, even those led by bourgeois nationalists, a greater degree of freedom to manoeuvre in their struggles. Liberation movements were able to hope and to fight for political and economic independence from imperialism as a first stage in improving the material conditions of the masses.

In this context left-wing forces within liberation movements wielded significant power. In relation to the Middle East US Secretary of State Warren Christopher admitted as much, asserting that the Soviet Union whilst it existed:

14 October, Stop Bombing Gaza protest, London.

'emboldened radicals, intimidated moderates and left Israel, save for the friendship of the United States, in a lonely state of siege.' (*International Herald Tribune*, 21 September 1993)

However, the collapse of the Soviet Union and the socialist bloc has enabled imperialism to decisively reassert unrivalled international economic, political and military power against all Third World opposition. In consequence, the dependent bourgeoisie, weakened by its own corruption and is own subordination to imperialist capital, has neither the ability nor the will to seriously oppose imperialism. In exchange for a few perks it shamelessly submits to imperial dictates whilst the conditions of the masses touch levels of unprecedented poverty and suffering.

The collapse of the Soviet Union and the onset of the new colonialism has highlighted once again the compromising and cowardly role of the bourgeoisie in the national struggle. James Connolly, a great Marxist and fighter for Irish national liberation murdered by the British in 1916, aptly noted that in the national struggle the working class cannot rely on 'the leadership of a class whose social character is derived from oppression.' All 'bourgeois movements end in compromise' and the 'bourgeois revolutionist of today becomes the conservative of tomorrow.' In the epoch of imperialism therefore, only 'the working class remains as the incorruptible inheritors of the fight for freedom.'

The cowardly role of the Palestinian bourgeoisie makes Connolly's standpoint particularly appropriate for Palestinian revolutionaries, For the sake of some minor neo-colonial economic and political privileges, the Palestinian bourgeoisie and its political representatives in the PLO have betrayed the interests of the masses. They have abandoned the struggle for a secular and democratic state across the whole of Palestine which could set the stage for real national and social emancipation for all the workers and peasants of the region — Arab or Jewish.

The future of the Palestinian revolution

For over five months the West Bank and Gaza Strip have been sealed off from Israel and from Jerusalem. Hundreds of thousands of Palestinians and their families who rely on slave labour in Israel for their meagre living are now desperately hungry. Imperialism, Zionism, Arab reaction and the PLO hope that the promise of international aid to release the masses from their desperate position will reconcile them to the neo-colonial autonomy plan and marginalise the opposition.

This task will not be easy. There have been numerous strikes and demonstrations against the deal. The left within the Palestinian movement, having withdrawn from the PLO, is organising against the sell-out. But confronted with the radical rhetoric of the fundamentalist forces, the left's fortunes will depend on how clearly and persuasively it can demonstrate that in this epoch the struggle for national liberation cannot be separated from the struggle for social liberation, that for success the struggle against Zionism and imperialism must be united with the struggle against capitalism.

The influence of Muslim fundamentalism among the poor and dispossessed of Palestine (see FRFI 113, February/March 1993) will seriously hinder the task of developing and consolidating an anti-imperialist and anti-capitalist opposition. Despite its radical rhetoric opposing the agreement, Hamas, the major fundamentalist organisation, is already engaged in secret negotiations with Al Fatah. It is not so much opposed to the deal as to the apportioning of the spoils. In any event, fundamentalism's opposition to the PLO has never had any revolutionary or democratic content. This is evident from its support for private property and capitalism, its programme for driving women out of social life and out of the liberation struggle, its virulent opposition to communism's democratic, collective and egalitarian standpoint and its sectarianism against Palestinian Christians.

The Palestinian revolution confronts difficult days ahead. The least we can do in Britain is to continue exposing the reactionary role of imperialism and Zionism is sustaining an order in the Middle East the end result of which is abject poverty, war and death for the majority, whilst enormous riches are siphoned off to feed the greed of a tiny rich minority in the imperialist heartlands.

chapter eleven

THE BRITISH LABOUR PARTY AND ZIONISM

▼ by *Steve Palmer*
from *FRFI No.29*, May 1983

The responsibility for establishing the Zionist state of Israel lies right here, in Britain. And the British Labour Party is the primary political instigator and supporter of the Zionist state. The 1917 Balfour Declaration of the British government supported the 'establishment in Palestine of a national home for the Jewish people'. Though the Balfour Declaration had been issued by Tories, it was rapidly endorsed by the Labour Party and the TUC in their 'War Aims Memorandum', adopted in December 1917:

> *'Palestine should be set free from the harsh and oppressive government of the Turk, in order that this country may form a Free State, under international guarantee, to which such of the Jewish people as desire to do so may return and may work out their salvation free from interference by those of alien race or religion.'*

The Declaration had several imperialist aims. One was an attempt to counteract the struggle by the Bolsheviks to overthrow the Russian government and take Russia out of the imperialist war then raging. A later Colonial Office memorandum, written for Winston Churchill in 1922 explained:

> *'The earliest document is a letter dated 24th April 1917 in which a certain Mr Hamilton suggested that a Zionist mission should be sent to Russia for propaganda purposes. It is clear that at that stage His Majesty's Government were mainly concerned with the question of how*

Russia (then in the first stages of revolution) was to be kept in the ranks of the Allies. At the end of April the Foreign Office were consulting the British Ambassador at Petrograd as to the possible effect in Russia of a declaration by the Entente of sympathy for Jewish national aspirations. The idea was that such a declaration might counteract Jewish pacifist propaganda in Russia.'

A memorandum from Ronald Graham, Assistant Under Secretary of State for Foreign Affairs to Lord Hardinge, Permanent Under Secretary, dated 13th June 1917, remarks:

'We ought therefore to secure all the political advantage we can out of our connection with Zionism and there is no doubt that this advantage will be considerable, especially in Russia ...'

The British imperialists were contemptuous of the indigenous Palestinian population – and said so quite openly to one another. Balfour explained in a Memorandum to Curzon that:

'In Palestine we do not propose even to go through the form of consulting the wishes of the present inhabitants of the country ... Zionism, be it right or wrong, good or bad is rooted in age-long traditions, in present needs, in future hopes, of far profounder import than the desires and prejudices of the 700,000 Arabs who now inhabit that ancient land.'

The Declaration had been made without reference to the Palestinian people, who overwhelmingly opposed it. It was therefore inevitable that a Zionist state in Israel would be a racist state, and an outpost of imperialism in the Middle East.

It was the racist British Labour Party which was to be the midwife to the birth of the Zionist state. This was the logical outcome of the strong Zionist ties and sympathies of the Labour Party, allied to its unswerving support for British imperialism. In 1920, Paole Zion, the British section of the International Organisation of Socialist Zionists, had affiliated to the Labour Party, and from the early twenties, the Zionist current in the party grew rapidly.

The central problem which taxed the Zionists, following the Balfour Declaration, was the need to build up the Jewish Zionist colony in

Palestine, the Yishuv: in 1918, Jews in Palestine – the supposed homeland – formed less than 10% of the Palestinian population. Without massive Zionist immigration into the country, the plan for a Zionist state would have collapsed. By 1929 the Jewish population had nearly trebled to 156,000. The Zionists owned 4% of the land, but 14% of the cultivable area. The Zionists, vigorously supported by their racist trade union Histradut, strictly enforced a policy of exclusively Jewish employment, both on the land and in industry.

The MacDonald letter

In August 1929, weeks after a new Labour Government had taken office, hundreds were killed and many more injured in violent riots in Jerusalem. A government enquiry showed that the root cause of the hostility between Palestinian Arabs and Jewish settlers was the expulsion of peasants from land acquired by the Zionists, and recommended curtailing further Zionist immigration. Labour Colonial Secretary, Lord Passfield (formerly Sidney Webb), issued a White Paper recommending caution over unrestricted immigration to Palestine.

The Zionists unleashed a storm of fury. The Labour Prime Minister, Ramsey MacDonald, took control of Palestine out of Passfield's hands and passed it over to a Cabinet committee which, jointly with the Zionist Jewish Agency, drafted a letter which MacDonald read to Parliament on 13 February 1931. The letter, addressed to Chaim Weizmann, the Zionist leader who was to become Israel's first President, overturned the White Paper:

> 'The obligation to facilitate Jewish immigration and to encourage close settlement by Jews on the land, remains a positive obligation of the Mandate, and it can be fulfilled without prejudice to the rights and position of other sections of the population of Palestine.'

It was a testament of Labour support for Zionism, and as Weizmann remarked, the reversal in policy had a decisive effect on the establishment of the state:

> 'It was under MacDonald's letter to me that the change came about

in the Government's attitude, and in the attitude of the Palestine administration, which enabled us to make the magnificent gains of the ensuing years. It was under MacDonald's letter that Jewish immigration into Palestine was permitted to reach figures ... undreamed of in 1930.'

MacDonald also expressed the Labour government's support for the Zionists' policy of apartheid in employment, which was directed against the Palestinian Arabs:

'It is necessary also to have regard to the declared policy of the Jewish Agency to the effect that in "all the works or undertakings carried out or furthered by the Agency it shall be deemed to be a matter of principle that Jewish labour shall be employed." His Majesty's Government do not in any way challenge the right of the Agency to formulate or approve and endorse such a policy.'

Labour's complete contempt for the Palestinian Arabs was further confirmed by another incident recounted by Weizmann:

'The first indication I had of the seriousness of MacDonald's intentions was when he consulted me with regard to the appointment of a new High Commissioner to replace Sir John Chancellor.'

There is no record that the Labour Party consulted the Palestinian Arabs, expelled from land acquired by Zionists, over who they would prefer as High Commissioner.

The First Intifada 1936-39

Throughout the 1930s, Arab resistance in Palestine to Zionist encroachment increased until it broke out into open rebellion against the British state in 1936. The rebellion began in April with the launching of a general strike which lasted six months. The British responded by dynamiting houses, criminalising freedom fighters, and killing 1,000 people. Even as the general strike was still in progress, the British Trades Union Congress (TUC), meeting in Plymouth, showed its racist support for Zionism and contempt for the Palestinians:

'The Congress earnestly hopes that the British Government … will take all the necessary measures to bring the present disorders to an end.'

The Government followed this advice. The rebellion was crushed after three years by 20,000 British troops who left more than 5,000 Arabs dead and 14,000 wounded.

A Zionist militia had been formed, armed and trained by the British, called the 'British Settlement Police'. It was similar in composition and purpose to the 'B Specials' or UDR in British-occupied Ireland, and by 1939 it numbered 21,500 Zionists – one in 20 of the Jewish population! The British also formed joint terror squads with the Zionists, similar to the SAS, known as the 'Special Night Squads'. Led by a British officer named Orde Wingate, these provided training for future members of the Zionist, terror gang known as the Irgun. The Zionist deputy head of these squads was Moshe Dayan, later to become notorious in the 1967 'Six-day War'. Dayan later, remarked:

'In some sense every leader of the Israeli Army even today is a disciple of Wingate. He gave us our technique, he was the inspiration of our tactics, he was our dynamic.'

After the rebellion was crushed, remaining opposition was further undermined by the policy spelt out in the Tories' 1939 White Paper. This recommended sharply restricted Jewish immigration, regulation of land sales, and rejected a Jewish state, holding out promises of Palestinian self-government in the future. At its May conference, the Labour Party condemned these immigration restrictions at a time when European Jews were being brutally massacred by fascism, but it became clear that this criticism was simply ammunition to further Zionist designs:

'This Conference reaffirms the traditional support given by the British Labour Movement to the re-establishment of a National Home for the Jewish people in Palestine. It recognises that considerable benefits have accrued to the Arab Masses as a result of Jewish immigration and settlement. This Conference is convinced that under the policy of the Balfour Declaration and the Mandate, the possibility exists for continued and increasing peaceful cooperation between the Jewish and Arab peoples in Palestine.'

1944: 'The Static Arab'

In December 1944, the annual Labour Party Conference passed its strongest pro-Zionist motion to date:

> 'There is surely neither hope nor meaning in a "Jewish National Home" unless we are prepared to let Jews, if they wish, enter this tiny land [Palestine, not Britain] in such numbers as to become a majority. There was a strong case for this before the war. There is an irresistible case now, after the unspeakable atrocities of the cold and calculated German Nazi plan to kill all Jews in Europe. Here, too, in Palestine surely is a case, on human grounds and to promote a stable settlement, for transfer of population. Let the Arabs be encouraged to ... move out as the Jews move in. Let them be compensated handsomely for their land and let their settlement elsewhere be carefully organised and generously financed. The Arabs have many wide territories of their own; they must not claim to exclude the Jews from this small area of Palestine, less than the size of Wales. Indeed we should reexamine also the possibility of extending the present Palestinian boundaries, by agreement with Egypt, Syria or Transjordan.'

The racism behind-this motion was made clear by its drafter, Hugh Dalton, later Labour Chancellor:

> 'In Palestine we should lean, much more [!] than hitherto towards the dynamic Jew, less towards the static Arab.'

This shameless racism proved embarrassing even for the Zionists. Commented Weizrnann:

> 'I remember that my Labour Zionist friends were, like myself, greatly concerned about this proposal. We had never contemplated the removal of the Arabs, and the British Labourites, in their pro-Zionist enthusiasm, went far beyond our intentions.'

The 1945 Labour Government

After the war, another Labour government was returned to power. Its policy towards Palestine was dictated by the Labour Party's concern to safeguard Britain's overall imperial interests. The war had weakened

10 November 2023, Protest outside Barclays Bank, London.

British imperialism. Britain had negotiated a massive dollar loan from US imperialism. Since Sterling could not be freely exchanged for other currencies, scarce US dollars had to be conserved to pay back the US imperialists. Since oil from the Middle East did not have to be purchased with dollars, the control and security of these resources was therefore of vital importance to British imperialism, quite apart from its energy needs. Bevin, the Foreign Secretary, expressed Labour's problem very clearly:

'His Majesty's Government must maintain a continuing interest in the area, if only because our economic and financial interests in the Middle East are of great importance to us and to other countries as well. I would like this fact faced squarely. If these interests were lost to us, the effect on the life of this country would be a considerable reduction in the standard of living. Other parts of the world would suffer, too. The British interests in the Middle East contribute substantially not

*only to the prosperity of the people there, but also to the wage packets
of the workers of this country. Nor can we forget our old and valued
friendships with the peoples of the area.'*

To defend its empire, the Labour government, as Bevin hints, attempted
to draw conservative elements of the Arab states into support for its
designs. From this perspective, the establishment of a Zionist state in
Palestine was – at this time – a threat to British imperialist interests.
Richard Crossman, strongly pro-Zionist, claims that this was because
Bevin identified Zionism with communism:

*'I tried to convince him that it was just because the leaders of the
Yishuv were of Russian origin that nearly all of them were fanatically
opposed to Russian Communism. Moreover, apart from a minority
of fellow travellers, I added, the leadership of the Histradut ... felt
that the one Labour movement in the world whose ideals they shared
was the British. But nothing could shake his idée fixe that the British
position in the Middle East ... was threatened by a Jewish-Communist
conspiracy ...'*

More plausibly, Mayhew, then Bevin's Under-Secretary, argues that
Bevin was opposed to a Zionist state because it would stimulate radical
nationalism in the Arab states which might be directed against imperialist
interests:

*'Its success would condemn the Middle East to decades of hatred and
violence, and above all – this was his immediate concern – that by
turning the Arabs against Britain and the Western countries, it would
open a highroad for Stalin into the Middle East.'*

Bevin's fears of communist influence in the Middle East were not
fanciful: the Labour government was already waging war against the
Greek people led by communists, and in Azerbaijan and Kurdistan
autonomous republics with Soviet backing had been established after the
war.

But the Zionists began a war of terror against the British in Palestine;
in the Labour Party, tension on the question mounted. Within the Cabinet
there was deep sympathy for the Zionists. At one point Richard Crossman

visited John Strachey, a member of the Cabinet Defence Committee, and asked his advice about an act of sabotage planned by his Zionist friends:

> *'The next day in the Smoking Room at the House of Commons, Strachey gave his approval to Crossman. The Haganah went ahead and blew up all the bridges over the Jordan.'*

It is impossible to imagine a British Cabinet approving a similar IRA operation!

Michael Foot

The political atmosphere inside the Labour Party can be gauged from a pamphlet which Michael 'Peacemonger' Foot wrote together with Crossman entitled A Palestine Munich. Dismissing any danger to the future Zionist state from the surrounding Arab states, the pamphlet remarks:

> *'There is nothing which any of these states can do in the nature of formal warfare either individually or collectively, that could not be countered by an airborne brigade or even an airforce demonstration.'*

The pamphlet explained the conflict in racist terms:

> *'Tribal, dynastic and religious antagonisms take more fanatical forms in the Oriental than in the Western world...*
>
> *... the liberal era has never dawned on these countries. Such political mass movements as exist have a closer resemblance to the mass movements of the European Middle Ages than to those of the era of enlightenment.'*

Although it might be expedient to preserve friendship with the states of the Arab League, this would backfire and threaten British imperialism:

> *'Once we had defeated the Jews for them, the Arabs would demand immediate withdrawal of our troops from Palestine, and stage a revolt if this were not conceded. Then the last base for the defence of Suez would have gone.'*

Far better to back the Zionist settlers and to partition the state:

> *'The government of the Judean State would be eager to negotiate a treaty of alliance with Great Britain ... such a treaty would leave in*

British hands the port of Haifa and such airfields and installations as
we require ... Britain would be in a far stronger position than she is
at present.'

In the event, it was the Zionist terror campaign, and not the danger
of nationalism or communism which threatened imperialist stability.
With the encouragement of US imperialism, the Labour government
announced that it would withdraw British troops from Palestine by 15
May 1948. The Labour Party breathed a sigh of relief, and Weizmann
remarked, 'Now, thank God, we can live on friendly terms.' Labour
had created Zionist Israel and paved the way for genocide against the
Palestinian people.

The terror squads were now turned on the Palestinian people. On 9
April 1948 the Irgun, led by Menachem Begin, conducted the massacre
of Deir Yassin, when the Zionists butchered 254 Arab men, women and
children in cold blood. This was only a particularly gruesome example
from a genocidal wave of terror which drove 900,000 of the 1,300,000
Arab population out of Palestine, and left the Zionists holding 77 % of
the land.

Suez 1956

With their state established, the Zionists began to threaten the countries
bordering their statelet, carrying out repeated attacks on them. When the
Egyptian leader Nasser requested arms from the United States to defend
his country, he was told he could have them provided that he joined the
US puppet states in the anti-Soviet Baghdad pact. Nasser refused and
negotiated for arms with Czechoslovakia. The US imperialists then
withdrew finance from the Aswan Dam project, vital to irrigating the
Egyptian land. On 26 July 1956, Nasser announced the nationalisation of
the Suez canal; instead of its revenues going to enrich imperialists, they
would be used to finance the Aswan Dam.

The British and French imperialists were up in arms. And so was the
'socialist' Labour Party which condemned the nationalisation as 'high-
handed and totally unjustifiable'. A week later, Labour leader Gaitskell

31 December, End British support for Zionism, North London 2023

likened Nasser to Hitler and Mussolini and called on the government to supply the Zionists with British arms. Labour also made it clear that it did not rule out the use of force.

Despite weeks of imperialist wheeling and dealing, it became clear that Britain and France did not have the support of the US to use force, while the socialist countries and oppressed nations were siding with Egypt. Labour became increasingly worried that the use of force might endanger imperialism's wider interests. This opposition was entirely limited to criticising the government's tactics, and had nothing to do with anti-imperialism.

On 12 September, Gaitskell told the Commons that:

'If the government do this, they will leave behind in the Middle East such a legacy of distrust and bitterness towards the West that the whole area will be thrust almost forcibly under Communist control. This is the greatest danger of all.'

The British and French secretly arranged for puppet Israel to invade Egypt at the end of October, so that they could intervene 'to keep the two sides apart' – in fact to attack the Egyptians. When the news of the British invasion broke, the Labour Party did not attack the violation of Egyptian freedom nor did it utter even a whisper against the slaughter of the Egyptian people. Instead it condemned the government for losing an opportunity to attack the socialist countries, threatened with counter-revolution in Hungary.

The British and French imperialists backed down after the US showed its opposition for its own imperialist reasons – and after the Soviet Union threatened Britain and France with rocket attack.

The Six Day War

In the 1960s, the Zionists staged a series of provocations against the Arab states. These reached a point where they could no longer be ignored, and Egypt, when it responded, was drawn into the carefully laid Zionist plans to occupy the Sinai and other territories. Nasser closed the Straits of Tiran on 22 May 1967. The British Labour Cabinet met the following day. According to Wilson, the Cabinet decided that:

'Though several ministers were committed friends of Israel and of Israeli leaders, we were all agreed to urge the utmost restraint, at a very difficult time, on her.'

In fact, the Labourites had decided to give the Zionists full imperialist backing. The same day, Abba Eban flew to London:

'From the airport in London, I drove with Ambassador Remez to Downing Street ...'

Wilson's reply was forthright. The Cabinet had met that morning and had reached a consensus that the policy of blockade must not be allowed to triumph; Britain would join with others in an effort to open the Straits.

Some 'restraint'! When George Thomson, Minister of State at the Foreign Office, was dispatched to Washington, he was accompanied by a senior member of the naval staff in order to co-ordinate British plans to open the straits with the Pentagon.

Labour's plans to send a British American naval force to sail through the Straits of Tiran had been delayed by the reluctance of the French imperialists to join in the adventure and was pre-empted by the Zionists' own attack on the Arab countries. Although the force never attempted to open the blockade, Labour had exhibited its usual enthusiasm for imperialist schemes. And this particular scheme had, without doubt, encouraged the Israelis to begin the Six-day War.

October 1973 War

In his book *The Chariot of Israel*, Harold Wilson explains the Labour Opposition's reaction to the war of October 1973, waged by the Arab states against Israel, and which threatened to liberate the Occupied Territories from Zionist rule:

> '*It was Labour who provided all the activity. As soon as the news of the invasion became known I telephoned the Israeli Ambassador ... I was in contact with him each day to hear of developments. The first thing he told me was that Mr Heath's Government had placed an embargo on the shipment of spares and ammunition to Israel needed for the Centurion tanks Britain had supplied when Labour had been in power. As soon as the Prime Minister, Edward Heath, returned to London, I went to No.10 to press him to change Government policy on spares and ammunition. When he refused, James Callaghan and I took up the issue publicly.*'

With such obliging support from the Zionist errand-boys of the Labour Party, it is a wonder that the Israelis bothered keeping their own Ambassador in London! Wilson goes on to quote the Israeli Foreign Minister, Abba Eban:

> '*The decision of Edward Heath and his government in London came as a specially harsh blow ... the British example affected other European countries ... It was only when Harold Wilson's Labour Government came to power that the scar in our relations began to heal.*'

Conclusion

This brief survey of recent Palestinian history shows Britain's responsibility for conceiving and nurturing the Zionist monster. It also exposes the key role consistently played by the Labour Party in this process throughout the entire period – at times even outdistancing the Zionists themselves. A golden testimony to services rendered by Labour comes from the late Zionist Prime Minister, Golda Meir:

> '*From the very beginning of the labour movement in Palestine we were in close contact with the international labour movement, with*

the British Labour Party, and Trades Union Congress in England, and with the labour federations in the United States. We believed in these organisations, in their programs and policies, and we were certain that they, above all, in moral sympathy with our purpose would help us.

'Probably one of the greatest factors in helping us to overcome our initial difficulties was the fact that from the very first, since 1917, we constantly received encouragement from the British labour movement and in later years from the American labour movement.'

It is true that recently there have been gestures of support for the Palestinians from sections of the Labour Party. At the 1982 Conference a motion was passed reversing the formal policy of the party. Dundee's Labour Council has flown the PLO flag at the City Hall. Such gestures deserve support.

Yet they do not represent a trend and may have been encouraged by less generous motives than solidarity. Support for the Palestinians can easily be reconciled with attempts to share in Arab countires oil wealth. Representatives of no less than 12 Arab oil states have been lured to Dundee in the hope of attracting investment and providing jobs for British workers. The fact is that today's Labour Party is true to its history. It is thoroughly pro-Zionist and pro-imperialist. Some 120 Labour MPs are members of the Labour Friends of Israel. Among the Zionists are many of the so called 'left', including Tony Benn and Eric Heffer. Another Labour MP is Greville Janner, who returned from a visit to Zionist occupied Lebanon, remarking that 'the soldiers' restraint has been remarkable'.

Opportunists like this form the core of the Labour Party and determine its political standpoint. The wretchedly pro-imperialist Labour Party did not call a single demonstration during last summer's Zionist butchery in Lebanon. Surely that says it all?

COMMUNISTS AND NATIONAL LIBERATION MOVEMENTS
same goal, different paths

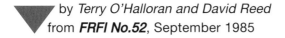 by *Terry O'Halloran and David Reed*
from **FRFI No.52**, September 1985

As communists in the world's oldest imperialist nation, the Revolutionary Communist Group (RCG) has consistently fought long and bitter struggles with the British left to establish the communist position of unconditional support for the struggle of national liberation movements against British imperialist domination and against national oppression. Our record on this, especially in relation to Ireland, is beyond serious challenge. In Britain, with its long tradition of imperialist exploitation, its strong and well entrenched labour aristocracy, communists have always had to emphasise the goal we have in common with the national liberation movements — the defeat of British imperialism.

As the crisis of British imperialism has deepened, with the consequent polarisation of British class society, and as the tempo of the national liberation struggles themselves has accelerated (Ireland 1981, South Africa 1984-5) inevitably the issue of the relationship between communists and national liberation movements will present itself in new ways, raising new questions and demanding answers. So today the very same political forces that yesterday accused the RCG of conceding to reactionary nationalism for demanding unconditional support for national struggles against British imperialism and against national oppression, are now flaunting a newly discovered 'solidarity' with liberation movements to justify their own opportunist attempt to sustain the deadly grip of the labour aristocracy over the working class and oppressed in Britain. It is, therefore, necessary to restate the basis of the communist standpoint on the national question.

Lenin and the right of nations to self-determination

Under imperialism the world has been divided into oppressor and oppressed nations and national oppression has been extended and intensified. A split has been created in the working class movement in the imperialist countries. One section, the labour aristocracy, has been corrupted by the 'crumbs that fall from the table' of the imperialist bourgeoisie, obtained from the super-exploitation and brutal oppression of the people from oppressed nations. The other, the mass of the working class, cannot liberate itself without uniting with the movement of oppressed peoples against imperialist domination. Only such an alliance will make it possible to wage a united fight against the imperialist powers, the imperialist bourgeoisie, and their bought-off agents in the working class movement. This means the working class fighting in alliance with national liberation movements to destroy imperialism *for the purpose of the socialist revolution*.

The unity of *all* forces against imperialism can only be achieved on the basis of the internationalist principle 'No nation can be free if it oppresses other nations'. This is expressed through the demand of the right of nations to self-determination. This demand recognises that class solidarity of workers is strengthened by the substitution of voluntary ties between nations for compulsory, militaristic ones. The demand for complete equality between nations, by removing distrust between the workers of the oppressor and oppressed nations, lays the foundation for a united international struggle for the socialist revolution. That is, for the only regime under which complete national equality can be achieved.

While the working class in the oppressed and oppressor nations have the same goal they necessarily approach it by different paths. As Lenin pointed out, the actual conditions of the workers in the oppressed and in the oppressor nations are not the same from the standpoint of national oppression. The struggle of the working class against national oppression has a twofold character:

*'(a) first, it is the "action" of the nationally oppressed proletariat and peasantry jointly with the nationally oppressed bourgeoisie against the oppressor nation; (b) second, it is the "action" of the proletariat, or of its class-conscious section, in the oppressor nation against the bourgeoisie of that nation **and all the elements that follow it.**'* (Lenin, A caricature of Marxism and imperialist economism, *our emphasis bold*)

Lenin was accused of being inconsistent in his attitude to nationalism for arguing that the approach of the working class in the oppressor nation to this question was necessarily different from that of the working class in the oppressed nation. His reply to his critics was simple and direct.

'Is the position of the proletariat with regard to national oppression the same in oppressing and oppressed nations? No, it is not the same, not the same economically, politically, ideologically, spiritually, etc.

'Meaning?

'Meaning that some will approach in one way, others in another way the same goal ... from different starting points.' (Lenin, The nascent trend of imperialist economism*)*

What this means is that the strategy and tactics necessary for building an effective anti-imperialist movement in Britain (the oppressor nation) may differ from the strategy and tactics required to develop the liberation movement's struggle in the oppressed nation. The RCG has long opposed all attempts by the British Labour movement and the British left to impose their own, usually opportunist, strategy and tactics on the liberation movement. Equally, the RCG is opposed to all attempts to impose the strategy and tactics developed by liberation movements to meet the specific conditions of their own struggles on the anti-imperialist movement in Britain. The example of the Lancaster House negotiations on Zimbabwean independence in 1979 makes this point clear. Communists in Britain defended the right of the Patriotic Front to enter into negotiations with and make concessions to the British government, whilst, at the same time, attacking the British government for imposing these concessions on the liberation movement.

Opportunists hide behind liberation movements

On the question of Ireland and South Africa opportunists are attempting to use Sinn Fein and the ANC to attack the RCG's approach to solidarity work. In a recent leaflet *Proletarian*, a tiny and uninfluential group associated with the *Morning Star*, attacks the RCG's work on Ireland using a quote from a review in the Sinn Fein journal *Iris* of I*reland, the key to the British revolution*. In the same leaflet it attacks the RCG's involvement in City of London Anti-Apartheid Group and demands the disbanding of City AA on the grounds of 'solidarity' with the ANC. Readers should note that *Proletarian* chooses to support the *Morning Star*, a newspaper which is vehemently opposed to the Irish national liberation struggle. This fact alone exposes the cynical and opportunist character of Proletarian's solidarity. We cite *Proletarian* only because it is a typical example of the way in which British opportunists use liberation movements for their own narrow sectarian ends.

The review referred to by *Proletarian* appeared in *Iris* No 10 July 1985. The review contains important distortions of the RCG's position on building a movement in Britain. (See review and our reply Fight Racism! Fight Imperialism! No 52, September 1985, on our website). More important for our argument here however, is the standpoint stated in the review on solidarity work and the strongly implied attitude of the reviewer that socialists in Britain should adopt the same standpoint. G McAteer accepts our central argument that emancipation of Ireland is a necessary precondition for the socialist revolution in Britain. We are also in agreement that socialists in Britain should 'build on whatever support there is in Britain for a withdrawal'. Where we disagree fundamentally with the reviewer is the assertion that the possibility of building an effective *anti-imperialist* solidarity movement in Britain 'is a totally unrealistic expectation given the political situation for the foreseeable future'. On the basis of this the review concludes that the RCG has adopted 'an isolationist stance that is doomed to obscurity' —the very quote seized upon by the truly obscure *Proletarian* sect.

This position ignores the political developments which have taken

24 October 1987, Anti-apartheid protest, London

place in Britain particularly in the last five years. During the crucial period of the hunger strike in 1981 major British cities saw the most significant, intense and wide-spread street confrontations between the oppressed black and white youth and the police. These were the most serious spontaneous revolts in Britain in the whole post-war period. The possibility of uniting the oppressed in Britain with the Irish people in a common struggle against a common enemy was there for all to see. The opportunity was thrown away precisely because the existing solidarity movement led by the Troops Out Movement turned its back on these developments for fear of disrupting its, in any case, futile attempt to win the official Labour movement to support the hunger strike. Rather than appeal to a section of the working class which had a common interest with the Irish people in defeating the Thatcher government and was actually fighting that government on the streets, the existing solidarity movement adapted its campaign to avoid any exposure of its chosen allies in the Labour Party: the very people who, in government, were responsible for the hunger strike —by withdrawing Special Category Status for political prisoners in 1976 —and who viciously condemned the risings in Britain.

The miners' strike 1984-5 once again demonstrated that the deepening British crisis would produce new forces that could be won to an anti-imperialist position on Ireland. The striking miners' experience of police brutality, government manipulation and rigged courts led many of them to identify their own struggle with that of the Irish people. The risings in 1981 and the miners' strike 1984-5 have already shown that the expectation that real possibilities for building an effective anti-imperialist movement exist in Britain is far from being 'unrealistic'. Indeed as the crisis develops and more and more sections of the working class are forced into confrontation with the British state these possibilities will multiply.

The growing political and social crisis in Britain has also revealed that the official Labour movement will move further and further to the right as its own position is increasingly threatened — a point confirmed during the miners' strike. What is indeed a 'totally unrealistic expectation' is any belief that the existing official Labour movement can be won to a progressive position on Ireland.

Comrade McAteer and the Republican Movement have every right to assess developments in Britain from their own standpoint and act upon that assessment. But neither the Republican Movement nor opportunists in Britain claiming to act in its name have any right whatsoever to demand that the RCG and other British anti-imperialists must accept that assessment and any conclusions that flow from it. For while we have the same goal as the Republican Movement — the defeat of British imperialism in Ireland —we necessarily approach that goal along a different path. Comrade McAteer is right to say that 'Republicans cannot afford the luxury of waiting around until the British working class becomes sufficiently politicised to fully support our struggle in all its form'. But we equally are right to expose the role of the official Labour movement and to fight against the very opportunism which not only obstructs the struggle for Irish self-determination but also the struggle for socialism in Britain. We are also right — indeed it is our duty —to concentrate our efforts on building an effective anti-imperialist movement amongst the most oppressed sections of the working class, whilst at the same time working in unity with any other forces whenever possible.

Similar issues have arisen in relation to the building of a solidarity movement against the apartheid regime. The *Proletarian* leaflet claims that Johnstone Makatini, Director of the ANC's International Department has called for 'the shelving of differences within the Anti-Apartheid

Movement in this country and for unity on the basis of exclusive recognition of the ANC'. This is a misrepresentation of comrade Makatini's remarks in London on 3 August. He did urge unity of the AAM in Britain. He did say as a separate point that the ANC had initiated a campaign for what he called, 'exclusive recognition' of the ANC as the sole representative of the liberation struggle in South Africa. If the ANC chooses to campaign for `exclusive recognition' that is a matter for the South African people to resolve. The same would be true if the Pan Africanist Congress, the Black Consciousness Movement, the UDF, AZAPO or any other force within the overall liberation movement took a similar stand. It is not a matter for the movement in Britain to decide or, even worse, cynically exploit for their own narrow sectarian ends. *Proletarian*'s 'interpretation' of comrade Makatini's remarks, in any case, flatly contradicts the AAM's own constitutional requirement:

> '*to cooperate with and support Southern African organisations campaigning against apartheid' (Clause 2c)*

The AAM's constitutional position is the only correct internationalist position for organisations in Britain. That the leadership of the AAM has consistently failed to abide by its own constitution on this issue is something that must be opposed. For British organisations to take it upon themselves to decide only to recognise one liberation organisation fighting apartheid and not others in the same fight is British imperialist arrogance and chauvinism of the worst kind. Our task in Britain is to give unconditional support to all organisations in their fight against apartheid in South Africa regardless of differences which may arise between different sections of the liberation movement.

Unity in the British AAM does not mean the shelving of differences. Unity means the democratically organised co-operation of different forces with different political standpoints in a common campaign against the apartheid regime and against British collaboration with that regime. When those in the AAM, who have attacked and disaffiliated City AA and also attacked the RCG's involvement in the AAM, call for 'unity', what they mean is the bureaucratic imposition of their own narrow sectarian prejudices on all anti-apartheid activists. No one seriously committed to the destruction of apartheid could submit to this demand. The fact that these sectarians attempt to use the heroic sacrifices of the South African people and the ANC to justify their own sectarian behaviour is an insult to the people of South Africa.

In the forefront of the sectarianism in the AAM is the Communist Party of Great Britain (CPGB) — primarily the *Morning Star* wing of that party. In common with their counterparts in the solidarity movement on Ireland, they have rejected any attempt to build an alliance with the newly emerging political forces in Britain. All their anti-apartheid activity is strictly confined to what is acceptable to maintain their alliance with sections of the official Labour movement. Their 'unity' requires the separation of apartheid in South Africa and racism in Britain, disaffiliation of City AA (now the largest active anti-apartheid group in the country), attempts to ban FRFI from official AAM pickets, bureaucratic manoeuvring against anyone 'suspected' of wanting an active movement, and a foul, non-stop campaign of rumour, gossip and lies to justify their own position. (See reports in this FRFI and recent issues.) Any movement in Britain which denies basic democratic rights to its own supporters cannot possibly be trusted to wage a consistent fight for the democratic rights of the people of South Africa.

1 January 1969, Battle of the Bogside, Ireland.

The political priority of the CPGB and its allies in the leadership of the AAM is the election of a Labour government under Neil Kinnock. They are prepared to subordinate the struggle against apartheid to this opportunist end. This is why they object to FRFI being sold on official AAM events because it contains material on Ireland and other issues which expose the reactionary character of their chosen allies. We remind these self-styled communists of Lenin's explanation of the task of the working class in the oppressor nation in relation to national oppression, which is to oppose:

'the bourgeoisie of that nation and all the elements that follow it"

The Labour Party's record on South Africa, and its record on Ireland, prove beyond dispute that it is one of the elements that follow the bourgeoisie.

As with Ireland, so with South Africa, unconditional solidarity with the struggle against national oppression does not and cannot oblige British communists to give up that struggle against British opportunism. Our job, as communists and anti-imperialists, working in the world's oldest imperialist nation, is to formulate the strategy and tactics appropriate to the building of an anti-imperialist movement in Britain in solidarity with all those fighting British imperialism and national oppression.

Suggested reading.

- **Lenin:** *'The nascent trend of imperialist economism'*, Collected Works, Volume 23
- **Lenin:** *'A caricature of Marxism and imperialist economism'*, Collected Works, Volume 23
- **Lenin:** *'The right of nations to self-determination'*, Collected Works, Volume 20
- **Lenin:** *'The discussion on self-determination summed up'*, Collected Works, Volume 22
- **Reed D:** *Ireland: the key to the British revolution*, Chapter 2
- **Brickley C, O'Halloran T, Reed D:** *South Africa: Britain out of apartheid: apartheid out of Britain*

www.REVOLUTIONARYCOMMUNIST.org/join

GET ACTIVE.

join a
FIGHT RACISM! FIGHT IMPERIALISM!
supporters' group

Throughout this pamphlet we have shown the relationship between British imperialism and the occupation and oppression of Palestine. We have explained that the Zionist state is crucial to defending British strategic interests in the Middle East and that the British Labour Party has always been a pro-imperialist and therefore pro-Zionist party. We now have to build an internationalist, anti-racist and anti-imperialist opposition to British imperialism's support for the Zionist state. This movement must stand unconditionally with the Palestinian resistance and against the Zionist occupation. It will oppose the imperialist Labour Party and will be an active and democratic movement on the streets and in our communities. It will be a movement for socialism and we all have a role to play as part of it. Contact us today to join your local Fight Racism! Fight Imperialism! supporters' group!

APPLY ONLINE QR code link above
EMAIL rcg@revolutionarycommunist.org
PHONE (+44) (0) 20 7837 1743
WRITE BCM Box 5909 London WC1N 3XX

Bulk orders of this pamphlet

You can help to get this pamphlet widely circulated by ordering bulk copies.

☐ 5 for £14.95 (inc P&P)

☐ 10 for £24.95 (inc P&P)

☐ 20 for £39.95 (inc P&P)

We hope that it will lead to reading groups in schools, colleges, universities, workplaces and communities. It is vital for the solidarity movement with Palestine to adopt an anti-imperialist position and arm itself with the ideas which are needed for this task.

Pay via PayPal at subscriptions@larkinpublications.co.uk

Or by cheque, payable to Larkin Publications. Add £5 for non-sterling cheques. FRFI BCM Box 5909, London WC1N 3XX

Order more copies of our publications

To order any of our pamphlets or books go to

www.revolutionarycommunist.org/shop

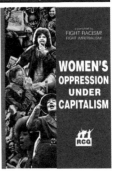

Subscribe to

FIGHT RACISM!
FIGHT IMPERIALISM!

www.REVOLUTIONARYCOMMUNIST.org

Keep up to date with our analysis. Subscribe to FRFI and visit our website!

FRFI SUBSCRIPTION RATES

	Biritain inc N.Ireland	Europe (air)	World (air)	PDF (email)
1 year	£10.00	£20.00	£25.00	£10.00
2 year	£18.50	£35.00	£48.00	£18.50

Pay via PayPal at subscriptiono@larkinpublications.co.uk
Or by cheque, payable to Larkin Publications. Please add £5 for non-sterling cheques.
FRFI BCM Box 5909, London WC1N 3XX

FRFI PRISONERS SUBSCRIPTION

PLEASE SUPPORT

Fight Racism! Fight Imperialism! is the only left newspaper in Britain which reports regularly on the struggles of prisoners. We send the paper free of charge to all prisoners who request it. Help this work, fund a subscription for a prisoner, follow the QR code link or check out our website.

	Biritain inc N.Ireland	World (air)
1 year	£20.00	£25.00
2 year	£35.00	£45.00